IMAGES
of Sport

MILLWALL
FOOTBALL CLUB
1885-1939

Jasper John Sexton, the first secretary of the newly formed Millwall Rovers. His father ran the Islanders beer shop in Tooke Street, the premises of which the fledgling club used as their headquarters and dressing rooms.

IMAGES
of Sport

MILLWALL
FOOTBALL CLUB
1885-1939

Compiled by
Chris Bethell, David Sullivan and the Millwall FC Museum

TEMPUS

First published 1999
Copyright © Millwall FC Museum, 1999

Tempus Publishing Limited
The Mill, Brimscombe Port,
Stroud, Gloucestershire, GL5 2QG

ISBN 0 7524 1849 1

Typesetting and origination by
Tempus Publishing Limited
Printed in Great Britain by
Midway Clark Printing, Wiltshire

Millwall Rovers, 1887/88. The team (photographed with the East End Cup) consists of, from left to right, back row: Mr Hughes, T. Jessop, H. Gunn, H. Butler, J. Meyers, Mr Henderson (secretary). Middle row: J. Shave, J. Fenton, J. Musgrove, T. Pitt. Front row: H. Warner, J. Reeves, D. Hean.

Contents

CAN YOU HELP
THE MILLWALL F.C. MUSEUM

The museum is being set up at the new
ground and we are collecting any
memorabilia on the Lions; photographs,
badges, programmes, newspaper
articles etc.
Photographs and newspaper cuttings
can be copied and returned.
All items used will be accompanied by
an inscribed plaque bearing the donors
name and dedication.
Anyone wishing to loan or exhibit
should contact the numbers below or
Deano Standing, Millwall F.C. Museum,
The Den, Zampa Road, SE16 3LN.
Items can also be handed in at offices,
clearly marked Millwall FC Museum.

Curators: R. Lindsay 081-698 0793 C. Bethell 081-395 6759
D. Sullivan 081-981 0567 E. Wilding 081-302 9355

Acknowledgements

On behalf of Millwall FC Museum, the authors would like to thank the following individuals and organisations, who have all been of assistance in the compilation of this book:

Bill Adams, the late Alf Amos, Steve Amos, Colin Atkins, John Ball, Mark Baxter, Bob Bennett, Andy Brewer, the late Bill Bryant, Denis Bryant, Michael Bryant, Muriel Clarke, Colorsport Photographic Agency, Richard Cooksey, Jim Creasy, G. Cross, Tony Davis, Chris Downham, Mark Eade, John Eustace, Benny Fenton, Mick Ford, Bill Foster, John French, Charlie Fuller, Allan Gillett, Peter Grace, Tom Green, John Hawkins, Pat Holmes, the late Frank Hookings, Island History Trust, Sid Jarvis, the late Jimmy Jinks, Tony Kentish, M. Kirkup, Jack Knapton, John Lloyd, Stan Locock, Peter Logan, Bert Mann, Len Mann, John Manning, Roy Marriott, Mark McAnnellan, Bob McCree, Kevin Meaney, Dave Murray, the late Joe Murray, Museum of London (Morton's Riverside), John Neale, Ian Page, Betty Phillips, the late George Phillips, Jim Phillips, the late Jimmy Pipe, Fred Reavell, Bryan Reynolds, Ryde Football Club, Colin Sayer, the Sexton family, Ken Sheehan, Anne Shiell, Rich Smart, Graham Smith, J.R. 'Reg' Smith, Tom Smith, John Stubbs, Dave Swannell, Bill Thompson, Denis Thorne and the Thorne family, Doreen Thorpe, John Thorpe, John Tye, Mike Walper, David Webster, Paul Wickes, Jamie Wiggins, Ted Wilding, Adrian Wisson, Roger Wood.

This book would not have been possible without Richard Lindsay.

Introduction

As far as anyone knows, Millwall Rovers was founded by workers of a local firm called C.&E. Morton & Co. in 1885, no doubt to keep some of the staff occupied on a Saturday afternoon. Following humble beginnings under the guidance of William Henderson, the club secretary, the newly formed outfit began to gain some eminence within the East End Football Association by winning the East End Cup three years in succession. The advances made since formation were at first gradual, but with the march of professionalism so prominent in the North and spreading down the country it was only a matter of time before the club took up the challenge themselves. Following an unsuccessful motion by Woolwich Arsenal to form a league of southern-based clubs, Millwall – with the word Athletic as a new suffix – turned professional in December 1893.

The outcome of several meetings was the formation of the Southern League – one that would hopefully attract the same amount of interest as that generated when the Football League was formed. Millwall Athletic's initiative to go ahead with this new competition was rewarded when they became champions in the inaugural season of 1894/95. Captain Alf Geddes, whose transfer from West Bromwich Albion had caused quite a stir in the Midlands when he came to London, played a major part in the success. Another championship followed in 1896, but thereafter the Dockers were never to win the Southern League title again (although it wasn't for want of trying with players such as Joe Gettins, John Calvey, Herbert Banks, Harry Matthew, Billy Stewart and George Henderson, who were all at the club in the late Victorian era). Millwall were given the chance to join the Football League in or around 1897, but this was turned down by the board because of the extra travelling and expense involved (although this hadn't stopped Woolwich Arsenal, even though they were based in an even more remote part of London).

Glory wasn't far away and fifteen years after they were founded, Millwall participated in their first FA Cup semi-final. However, within a year of losing to Southampton in 1900 a crisis loomed when, due to expansion of the dock system, Millwall were in danger of going out of existence, with most of the players going elsewhere to ply their trade. Fortunately, a last minute reprieve saw them acquire a piece of land along the East Ferry Road, which would be known as the North Greenwich ground and would be the club's home for nine years. With the threat of closure lifted Millwall could once again concentrate of football matters and try and recapture some of the glory won in the mid-1890s.

Millwall, once again under the captaincy of Ben Hulse, reached the FA Cup semi-final for the second time in 1903. This time it was Derby County who ended their dreams of greatness by winning 3-0 at Villa Park and again this setback seemed to retard Millwall's progress to becoming a great club: the expanding Southern League fixture list was met with apathy by the spectators who only looked forward to their yearly diet of FA Cup games. A highlight of this opening decade of the twentieth century was the winning of the first ever London Challenge Cup in 1909. By this time, Millwall had outgrown North Greenwich and the club was looking for pastures new to expand and attempt to increase revenue. As land was at a premium on the Island, the board looked south of the river for a spot in which to put down the club's roots. They found such a location at Cold Blow Farm where, under the watchful eye of Elijah Moor, a band of willing workers set out to build yet another ground, this time bigger and better than the site they had just vacated.

In October 1910, Millwall, who had taken the nickname 'the Lions', opened their new ground, The Den, for a match against Brighton & Hove Albion (who spoiled the party by winning 1-0). At end of that first season, even if the football being played wasn't much to write home about, the move appeared to be vindicated when the annual report was issued with favourable financial results. In its early days the new ground played host to a number of prestigious representative games, the biggest being an international match between England and Wales in March 1911. When the 'settling in' process at The Den was over it became a home from home for most diehard Millwall supporters and nearly every opponent hated having coming to it – not only would they face a committed Millwall side, but also a ferocious and passionate crowd who could generate a noise that could raise the hairs on the back of the neck: on many occasions such an atmosphere would turn the game in Millwall's favour. Despite the supporter's reputation as being highly committed, the reason for their passion has to come from the players on the pitch and in the years before the First World War inspiration came from Wally Davies, the Welsh international whose goals won many a match, Bert Lipsham's exciting wing play, the hard tackling and energy of Sammy Frost and the veteran Bert Moody (who played before and after the war, going on to team up with the freescoring Jimmy Broad).

During the 1920s the fortunes of the club took a turn for the better, the only minor blips occurring when the Lions were knocked out of the FA Cup by some of the lesser lights of English soccer. Overall, Bob Hunter got the side playing the kind of football that comes along once in a blue moon and when the Lions achieved their goal of Second Division football in 1928 they had hit a staggering 127 goals (a record for Division Three (South)) and had a team that many oldtimers would say was the finest in the club's history. Indeed, there were many remarkable players in that side: full-backs Jack Fort and Dick Hill (who were both capped by England), half-backs Amos Bryant and Graham (another England player) and forwards of such calibre as Jack Cock, Landells, Chance, Black, 'Peanut' Phillips and, no less important, goalkeepers Lansdale, Crawford and Fox.

When Bob Hunter passed away in 1933, the loss to the club was immense. This may have been one of the reasons that a year later Millwall suffered their first ever relegation, that even the great Bill McCracken, Hunter's successor, couldn't avoid. The club remained in the doldrums for the next three seasons until Charlie Hewitt arrived like a breath of fresh air to the environs of New Cross. He cleared away the cobwbs of depression, changed the colour of the team shirt and added a rampant lion badge to instill some pride in the players as they donned their kit. The effect was remarkable as the Lions roared to the semi-final of the 1937 FA Cup and were promoted back to Division Two the following year. To Lions everywhere it appeared that the club had found a new saviour and that Charlie Hewitt could walk on water – he probably could have, that is until Mr Hitler put an almighty spanner in the works.

This pictorial Millwall Football Club story will be continued in a second volume from Tempus Publishing, which will be available for Christmas 2000.

One
The Islanders
1885-1910

The East End Football Association Senior Challenge Cup, which was won by Millwall Rovers in 1887, 1888 and 1889. After these victories the club were allowed to keep the trophy – which is still in the possession of the present day Millwall Football Club.

The riverside frontage of C. & E. Morton's factory. This was the local firm whose employees had a lot of involvement with the formation of Millwall Rovers.

Millwall Rovers, *c.* 1889. From left to right, back row: Dr Murray Leslie, T. Jessop, H. Warner (vice-captain), J. Fenton, P. Smith, J. Morgan, J. Myerscouch, Mr W. Henderson. Front row: J. Tyler, J. Rowland, H. Butler (captain), G. Warner, N.Q. McFie.

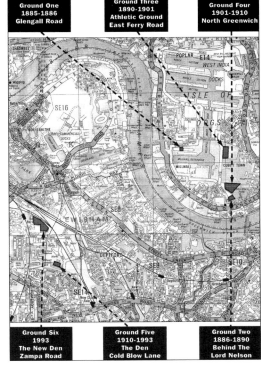

Ground One
1885-1886
Glengall Road

Ground Three
1890-1901
Athletic Ground
East Ferry Road

Ground Four
1901-1910
North Greenwich

Ground Six
1993
The New Den
Zampa Road

Ground Five
1910-1993
The Den
Cold Blow Lane

Ground Two
1886-1890
Behind The
Lord Nelson

This map shows the various grounds that the club has occupied since their formation in 1885.

MILLWALL ATHLETIC
v.
UXBRIDGE.

BRAVO Peter! your turn has come
 For notice in these lines,
Although your play has surely been
 Acknowledged many times;
Not one of our supporters can
 Dispute your reputation,
Kind words are said all round the ground
 Of your determination.
So let us hope that we shall see you
 Rise in our estimation.

J.W,R.

MILLWALL.

GOAL
CAYGILL
BACKS
LINDSAY   HARTUNG
HALF-BACKS
THOMPSON   BUTLER(cap)   **FENTON**
FORWARDS
M'CULLOCH JONES   BANKS   WITHINGTON GLOAK

~~~~~~~~~~~~~~~~~~~~~~~~~~~~~~~

A. WOODBRIDGE LENO   DENINGTON E WOODBRIDGE V GAYLARD
FORWARDS
BORTON R. WOODBRIDGE   WEST
HALF-BACKS
BROWN   GAYLARD
BACKS
STEVENS(cap)
GOAL

UXBRIDGE.

This is the oldest surviving match programme of Millwall Athletic, dated 30 October 1891. Athletic won this match with Uxbridge, their Middlesex rivals, 6-1.

Millwall Athletic FC, c. 1890. From left to right, back row: F.B. Kidd (treasurer), C. Squire (referee), W. Ingram (centre half), H. Lindsay (right full-back), J. Fenton (left half-back), H. Earle (left full-back), D. Gloak (outside left), O. Caygill (goalkeeper), W. Henderson (honorary secretary). Front row: F. McCulloch (outside right), E. Jones (inside right), H. Thompson (right half-back), P. Banks (centre forward), F. Withington (inside left).

A drawing showing the Millwall Athletic side taken from *Paddock Life* magazine of Tuesday 5 December 1891.

Millwall Athletic FC, 1891/92. From left to right, back row: Mr F.B. Kidd, H. Lindsay, T. Willing, G. Burton, H. Earle, O. Caygill, D. Gloak, Mr S.R. Carr (referee). Middle row: F. McCulloch, E. Jones, H. Butler (captain), F. Withington, P. Banks. Front row: H. Thompson, J. Fenton.

This *Penny Illustrated* drawing of 1 October 1892 depicts Millwall's 2-1 victory over Ilford at the East Ferry Road.

For Best and Fullest Football Reports see the "SPORTSMAN."

CHESHAM

GOAL — SELLS
BACKS — DARVELL, WOODS
HALF-BACKS — MOULDER, BARNES, MEAD
FORWARDS — SPRATLEY, MAYO, STONE, CULVERHOUSE, HOLLIMAN

THE champions of the Winter Sport
    Began their season well,
By beating Folkestone seven to one
    Of their prowess I must tell;
Their first goal was gained by Duke
    Who showed himself up grand,
Next Cunningham and Jones came off.
    Three to one the game did stand.

The superiority of the Athletics
    Added four goals to the score,
While Folkestone felt downhearted
    They could not get one more.
"WE ARE SEVEN" has been the cry,
    And heartily I quote it,
The first victory of the season
    And I feel bound to note it.

Sherwood Foresters should have come
    To face us here to-day,
But through the autumn manœuvres
    Are forced to stay away.
Chesham ably fills the place
    And glad we are to meet them,
I tell you plainly in this rhyme
    Millwall are sure to beat them.
            J.W.R.

MILLWALL ATHLETIC.

GOAL — FENN
BACKS — WILLING, DAVIES v.cap
HALF-BACKS — ROBERTSON, J. LINDSAY, DUKE
FORWARDS — A. WILSON, E. JONES, D. CUNNINGHAM, F. HOLLANDS, AITKEN

The "SPORTSMAN" Enlarged Edition every Monday.

A programme for the match against Chesham on 9 September 1893. This game finished as a 17-0 home victory – still the highest in Millwall's history for any type of match.

Millwall Athletic, 1893/94 season. From left to right, back row: W. Lindsay, J. Graham, W. Davis, G. Aitken, J. Duke, J. Robertson, O. Caygill (captain), A. Roston-Burk (referee). Front row: A. Wilson, E. Jones, J. Lindsay, W. Cunningham, F. Hollands.

Englifh Sports

No. 73. Vol. II. OCTOBER 7, 1893. PRICE ONE PENNY.

SOLE AGENTS FOR AUSTRALASIA AND AFRICA—ROBERT A. THOMPSON & Co., SYDNEY, MELBOURNE, ADELAIDE, BRISBANE, AND CAPE TOWN.

MILLWALL ATHLETICS.

A CHAT CONCERNING A RISING CLUB.

When the history of '93 football comes to be written, the scribe will in duty bound be compelled to mention the name of one club which, in the course of a few months, jumped from the lower rungs of the ladder of fame to nearly the top-most pinnacle. And the club? The Millwall Athletic. Few of those present at the memorable match played at Leyton on January 21st, between the Old Carthusians and the Millwallers, in which contest the latter were out-played to the tune of ten goals to one, anticipated that so sound a defeat would be the making of the losers. So it proved, however, for it showed the weak points in their armour. Setting to work in a thoroughly business-like manner, the executive rectified the failings, filled omissions, and as a sequence were enabled to meet and beat those important clubs with whom they had previously arranged fixtures.

The Millwall's concluding match of last season was, as the reader is no doubt aware, with West Bromwich Albion, a team by no means to be despised or called second-rate; ex-cupholders are in general reckoned of good standing. However, the Millwall Athletic, instead of obtaining the thrashing confidently promised them by the friendly Southern press, wound up a most unequal season of disaster and success by beating their powerful opponents. One goal to nothing is, perhaps, not a big win, but, had the West Bromwich Albion gained that solitary point to Millwall's duck's-egg, there's no doubt the knowing ones would, with up-lifted eyebrows, have murmured something about the visitors only just managing to get home.

This season the club has done even better. Their opening match (against Folkestone) they won by seven goals to one, then came their crushing defeat of Cheaham by seventeen goals to nil, on the following Saturday they provided what without doubt will be the surprise-packet of Southern '93-'94 football—we refer to their victory over the cup-holders, Wolverhampton Wanderers, by three goals to two.

People, not being able to recognise the sudden transition of the Millwall from moderate to first-class form, descried the Londoners' efforts, saying that, had they wished, the champions could have won easily. The question which naturally presents itself to the mind is—Why didn't they make the attempt and succeed? It certainly did the visiting team no good to receive a defeat. No; the actual truth is that both teams did their best, and Millwall won.

THE SKIPPER-CUSTODIAN.

Anxious to get a few authentic particulars of the hopes and prospects of the club, the writer managed to button-hole Mr. O. Caygill on Saturday, and put a few pertinent questions to him; for, as captain, he would be most likely to know the ropes. En passant, it has always been a source of wonderment to the SPORTS man that Caygill has not more often been invited to participate in some of our inter-county and other important matches. That he can play, we know! but why he has not figured, or, rather, been allowed to figure, more prominently, we don't know.

The portrait we give of him shows him attired in the costume that, until the present season, constituted the club's regulation pattern—blue and white stripes. Now, however, a much neater and uncommon guise is adopted, consisting of a close-fitting dark blue vest, with the same coloured knickers, a broad white stripe down the sides thereof relieving the monotony of the blue. We ment on their attire thus particularly, as its general appearance strikes the eye as being in keeping with their name "Athletic," for each man presents a clean limbed, smart figure.

To revert to Caygill. His tall, lithe form—he stands about six feet in height—is well-known down on the Island; his connection with the club now extends to four years, and under his captaincy the team has won its way to

O. CAYGILL (CAPT.).

the front. He has youth on his side, having begun his earthly career on the 2nd November, 1870, being thus only in his twenty-third year.

For seven years he has been sweet on leather, as far as that material extends to footballs, and at one time affected a position on the field other than that he now occupies. There is little doubt, however, he has found his proper post as goal keeper, and may he long continue to act as such.

On two occasions he has appeared in important combinations. The first was for London against Sheffield two years since, and the second was for Middlesex v. Kent. By the way, speaking of Sheffield, it brings to mind that as an outcome of the match the Sheffield United tried to induce him to turn "pro," but Caygill didn't quite see it. Previous to that, in 1890, the Royal Arsenal used

their best endeavours to get him to throw in his lot with them. Caygill is content to remain as he is an amateur playing the game for the game's sake, and not throwing up a good situation for a practically brief career as a professional.

Caygill's allusion to his temptations brought to, the SPORTS man's mind the oft-repeated assertion that the Millwall team is not a bona-fide amateur one. The question being put to him as to the grounds for the assertion, "All bosh!" was the captain's expressive reply. "Neither," he added, "is there any prospect of the club turning professional."

THE PAST AND THE FUTURE.

The writer then changed the conversation by asking a few questions as to the origin of the club. Like most things, it began uneventfully. A few tinsmiths, engaged on the Island, were the founders. First called the "Iona," it grew in importance until it reached its present position. The ground on which they now play was taken in 1890; originally a veritable swamp, by care and the expenditure of a goodly sum, a satisfactory field has been created.

It still continues practically a working-men's team, only one or two of its members being engaged in other occupations, such as clerkships; and it reflects every credit on their trainer, Lindsey, that the men turn out so fit as they do. There is a fine prospect before the club if no desertions occur, for the average age of the players is but twenty-two, and the combination is now reaching that perfection so essential to success. In the past, the defence was their weak point, but in Graham and Davies (of course with Caygill in goal) the club have found powerful and smart backs. Duke, Robertson, and Aitken want a lot of getting by; in fact, they are a trinity of excellent half-backs. So, too, with their forwards; Hollands, Cunningham, Lindsay (not their trainer, but a namesake), Jones, and Wilson, if light in build, make up for it by their speed and cleverness.

Caygill is of opinion that he has now a set of players equal to any in the South of England. He is sanguine of getting through the season in a satisfactory manner, and a good start has certainly been made; no defeats, and a goal total of 38 for 4 against. Last season they played 46 matches, winning 28, losing 11, and drawing 7, with 146 goals to their credit, and 77 against. They have a list of good engagements made out, but they would have dearly liked a tussle with the Arsenal, with whom they are in friendly rivalry. A couple of fixtures were indeed arranged, but the Reds cancelled them to meet League teams. They have entered for the English Cup, and it will be no fault of the Millwall if they do not render a good account of themselves.

This is probably the first front page article devoted to Millwall; it appeared in October 1893 on the front cover of *English Sport* and highlights the question of the Dockers' status – amateur or professional? This had been an ongoing debate since 1890 when Millwall had changed their name from Rovers to Athletic.

Obed Caygill, the first of many great Millwall custodians. Caygill was born in Southwark but played most of his football in Poplar. During his brief career he was coveted by some of the Football League clubs, but remained loyal to Millwall only to break a leg against Stoke in the very last match of the 1893/94 season. This injury forced Caygill to retire from the game he loved, although he didn't sever his connections with Millwall and his future input was to produce a team-sheet on matchdays.

Millwall Athletic, 1894. From left to right, back row: W. Lindsay (trainer), Mr N. Whittaker, W. Davis, G. Aitken, T. Walker, J. Matthews, H. Matthews, Mr E. Clark, H. Robertson. Front row: W. Jones, J. Wilson, J. Graham, A. McKenzie, A. Geddes.

Two of Millwall's finest in their Sunday best. *Left*: Skipper Jack Graham. *Right*: Colin Gordon was the club chairman during the 1890s. A chemist by profession, he was taken ill after a trip abroad and died in Guy's Hospital in 1910.

Millwall Athletic team from the Easter tour during the 1894/95 season. From left to right, back row: J. Wilson, J. Matthews, W. McNiven, O. Caygill, W. Davis, Mr G.A. Saunders. Middle row: Mr F.B. Kidd, W. Lindsay (trainer), G. King, W. Almond, Mr E.R. Stopher, H. Matthews. Front row: W. Jones, A. Simms, A. Robertson, A. McKenzie, A. Geddes.

Above: The Lord Nelson hasn't changed that much from the time Millwall Rovers used it as their base (from 1886-1890). The public house is located only 400 yards or so down the East Ferry Road from where the pitch would have been. This photograph was taken in 1990. *Below*: From 1890 until 1901, the George Hotel became the club's headquarters until suitable facilities were built at the spacious new athletic ground on the East Ferry Road.

John Graham was a native of Derby who was brought to London at an early age and, like many of his era, sport would play a major part in his upbringing; not only was Jack a fine footballer, but he excelled at sprinting and as a wrestler. This fine athlete (who was an impressive 6ft 1½ inches and 13st 10lb) came to Millwall from Cray Wanderers in around 1892 and went on to form a very impressive full-back partnership with 'Wiggy' Davis. Jack would play in over 80 games for the club over a six-season period. Later in his career he served Woolwich Arsenal and Brentford. The old saying 'Keep it on the island' that used to be heard at football matches can be attributed to Jack when Millwall played at East Ferry Road, for it was his long kicking that was the inspiration for the expression. Jack Graham died at Catford in 1925.

When Millwall signed Alf Geddes from West Bromwich Albion it was the action of a club that meant business. Alf was the first professional of note to appear for the club and was made skipper, although he played in the somewhat isolated position of outside left. He had been a hero at Albion, where he had won an FA Cup winner's medal when they beat rivals Aston Villa in the final, and it didn't take long for the locals on the Isle of Dogs to take a liking to him as well. Small in stature, his build in no way hampered his ability to strike fear into his opponents with his speedy running and awesome shooting. In his five seasons at the East Ferry Road, Alf played in 148 games and scored 59 goals. He went on to join fellow Southern Leaguers Bedminster (Bristol City) and the last club he signed for was Bristol Rovers in 1901.

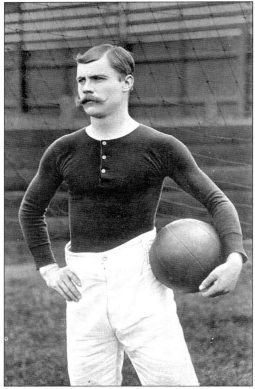

A Millwall team group posing with the Southern League Shield, 1896/97. From left to right, back row: Mr C. Gordon, Mr J.B. Skeggs, J. Curley, D. Robson, Mr E.R. Stopher, J. Graham. Third row: Mr J. Beveridge, Mr G.A. Saunders, Mr T. Thorne, Mr F.B. Kidd, Mr Higson. Second row: S. Hunt, G. King, A. Millar, H. Matthew, T. Moore, Mr E. Clark. Front row: M. Whelan, J. Calvey, J. Davies, A. McKenzie, A. Geddes. Millwall finished second in the Southern League, winning 13, drawing 5 and losing 2, scoring 63 and conceding 24 goals. John Calvey top scored with 17.

Millwall Athletic, 1898/99 season. From left to right, back row: D. Gow, C. Burgess, W. Allen, W. Davis, J. Graham. Middle row: R. Hunter, G. Crawford W. Stewart (captain), A. Millar, E. Moor. Front row: F. Morrison, J. Calvey, C. Hogan, P. Turnbull, A. Geddes. Millwall finished the season in third position in the Southern League, having won 12, drawn 6 and lost 6 of their games, scoring 59 goals and conceding 35. Peter Turnbull was the top scorer with 14.

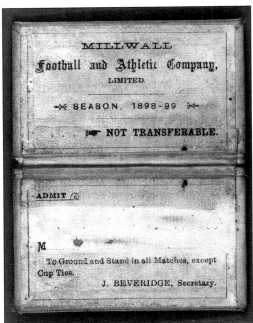

An outer cover (left) and inner detail from a season ticket for 1898/99. Understandably, these items are now very rare.

Millwall St Johns were eventually adopted by Millwall Athletic as their reserve team. The 1898/99 season was an excellent one for this local side – they played 30 games and won all of them, scoring 212 goals and conceding only 13. The team that carried off this remarkable achievement consisted of, from left to right, back row: Mr F. Thorne, Mr J. Griffith, E. Moor, F. Hasted, J. Jordan, Mr E. Stopher, D. Clear, W. Fenn, A. Fenn, C. Pettit, Mr Ball, Mr Bugg. Middle row: R. Riley, J. Bugg, W. Ainsworth. Front row: D. Maher, J. Hunt, E. Miller, R. Jones, H. Squires.

Willie Jones was one of three footballing brothers to play for Millwall (the others were called Eddie and Dick). Willie had two spells at the East Ferry Road. Tragically, in the process of scoring the winning goal for Ryde in the semi-final of the Isle of Wight Senior Cup in March 1899, he sustained an injury that proved fatal. He was buried in the local cemetery in Ryde.

Millwall Athletic won the Southern League Shield again in 1900. *Above*: The team pictured with the trophy. From left to right, back row: J. Hunt, R. Donkin, Mr F. Thorne, D. Clear, W. Davis, W. Ross. Middle row: Mr G.A. Saunders, J. Riley, J. Bugg, W. Squires, Mr E.R. Stopher, E. Moor. Front row: D. Mayer, J. Miller, F. Beven, R. Jones, W. Squires. *Left*: Directors G.A Saunders, F. Thorne JP and E.R. Stopher pose with the trophy. Note the impressive flag with the Millwall Athletic logo that has been used as a backdrop for both these photographs.

Millwall reached their first FA Cup semi-final in 1900. Their route to the last four in the competition took them past Clapton (7-0 in the third qualifying round), Chatham (3-0), Thames Ironworks (2-1), Jarrow (2-0 in the first round proper) and Queens Park Rangers (2-0). The third round put them against Aston Villa, the current League Champions. The much-fancied Midlanders took in lead in the first match at Millwall until Scot Dave Nicol equalised with a few minutes left. This sent the game back to a replay at Villa Park, which finished 0-0 after extra time. The third match was held at Reading and it was a great day for Millwall as they completed a famous 2-1 victory. Unfortunately, Millwall bowed out in the semi-final to Southampton (0-0 at the Crystal Palace and then 3-0 in the Reading replay). These action shots from the Aston Villa tie come from the *Illustrated Sporting and Dramatic News*. *Right*: The opposing captains at the toss. *Below*: The players awaiting an Aston Villa corner kick.

THE COCK O' TH' SOUTH.
The Southern Leaguers have a mighty big crow over the present League Champions.

This is how the cartoonist at the *Athletic Chat* saw the outcome of the second replay at Reading. The venue for the match was very convenient as it enabled Millwall to field the famous amateur J.H. (Joe) Gettins, who held a teaching post in the town. Gettins scored one of the goals in the famous 2-1 victory, the other being taken by Herbert Banks. Banks, who had matinee idol looks and excellent finishing, scored a total of 9 goals during the cup run. This brought him to the attention of the England selectors and a year later he was chosen to face Ireland at Southampton, thus becoming Millwall's first England cap.

Millwall Athletic pictured with the Southern Charity Cup. From left to right, back row: Mr Leavy, G. Burgess, Mr Stopher, W. Cox, Mr Colin Gordon, E.M. Allen, Mr J. Higson, Mr J. Beveridge. Third row: R. Hunter, Mr J.B. Skeggs, D. Smith, H. Goldie, A.T. Miller, Mr G.A. Saunders. Second row: W. Dryburgh, J. Brearly, J.H. Gettins, H.E. Banks, D. Nicoll. Front row: A. Caie, H. Robertson.

Millwall used two grounds in 1901. One of them was on the East Ferry Road and the other was at North Greenwich. Elijah Moor, the groundsman, organized the labour for the building of the North Greenwich enclosure as well as The Den in 1910. Even the players assisted in the construction of the ground at North Greenwich in the summer of 1901.

Millwall faced Southampton at Crystal Palace in the semi-final on 24 March 1900. A crowd of 34,760 watched the two teams play out a 0-0 draw. *Left:* Millwall's Millar shadows the Saints' left winger. *Right:* Durber of Southampton about to send the ball into the Millwall penalty area from a free kick.

Banks and Brearley are caught offside during the match.

MILLWALL F.C.

Opening of the New Ground, East Ferry Road, Millwall,

Wednesday, Sept. 18th,

MILLWALL
V.
ASTON VILLA.

KICK-OFF 4 O'CLOCK.

Admission, 6d. Ladies & Boys, 3d Stand, 6d. extra.

The Ground is situate within five minutes walk of North Greenwich Station and Pier.

Omnibuses from Poplar Station (N. L. R.) and West India Dock Station to the Ground.

There was no fanfare for the opening of the new East Ferry Road ground on 18 September 1901, just this small advertisement placed in the local newspaper, the *East End News*.

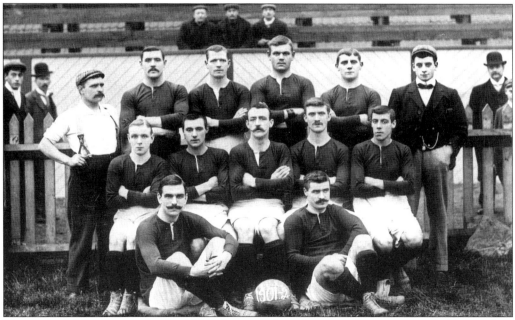

This is the Millwall team for the 1901/02 season that played on the new grounds. From left to right, back row: R. Hunter, W. Halley, J. Bell, J. Joyce, A Dunn, D. Maher. Middle row: J. Hamilton, J. Riley, B. Hulse, C. Dove, J. Kirton. Front row: J.H. Gettins, E. Watkins. Millwall finished the season in sixth position in the Southern League, having won 13, drawn 6 and lost 11 of their games, scoring 48 goals and conceding 31. Ernie Watkins was the top scorer with 14.

A full page spread on Millwall from the *Daily Express*, 18 October 1902.

THE FOOTBALL ASSOCIATION CUP.—MILLWALL AND BRISTOL ROVERS
PLAY A SECOND DRAW IN THIS COMPETITION, SO RENDERING A THIRD MATCH NECESSARY.

1. Cartledge stops a shot from Millwall.   2. Bristol go away at the start.   3. A corner to Millwall.   4. Cartledge saves for the Rovers.

Millwall Athletic went on another FA Cup run in the 1902/03 season. This page from *The Illustrated Sporting and Dramatic News* of 27 December 1902 shows the highlights of the first round replay against Bristol Rovers. This match was played at Millwall, the teams having already drawn 2-2 in Bristol. This game finished goal-less and the tie was decided in a second replay at Villa Park, which the Dockers won 2-0.

Having disposed of Rovers, Millwall went on to face fellow Southern Leaguers Luton in the first round proper. A crowd of 8,826 turned up at the North Greenwich enclosure to witness a 3-0 win for the home team. Preston North End were the subsequent opponents in the competition and the Dockers thrashed the northern side 4-1. Over 12,000 turned up to North Greenwich for this FA Cup second round fixture. *Above*: Preston defenders are all at sea after a Millwall corner. *Below*: McBride, the Preston goalkeeper, comes out to save.

Millwall faced Everton at home in the third round and beat them 1-0 in muddy conditions on 7 March 1903. A contemporary newspaper reported on the match as follows 'With the foothold so treacherous effective combination was out of the question, and in a scrambling game the Dockers were the better team. Their one goal was no doubt somewhat lucky, the greasy ball slipping through Whitley's fingers, but on the other hand Storrier only hit the crossbar with a penalty kick that was given them. Sutcliffe gave a superb display in goal, and the defence was generally very sound, while forward little Moran was a continual thorn to the Everton backs, and was, indeed, the best wing on the field'. *Above*: A tussle in midfield (Millwall are in white). *Below*: Millwall repel an Everton attack from a corner. This action shot shows Sutcliffe and his full-backs Easton and Storrier.

This action shot shows Millwall's best chance in the semi-final against Derby County at Villa Park. The Dockers started the game brightly, forcing several corners that were accurately centred by Moran, with the ball being headed just over the bar several times. However, the outcome of the match was effectively settled in the first quarter of an hour when Derby scored two goals in quick succession. The first was quite remarkable, as Derby half-back Warren received a pass back from a throw in and volleyed the ball high into the Millwall area. Sutcliffe ran out to catch it and, whether through sheer misjudgement or being blinded by the sun, came out too far and the ball went over his head and dropped into the net – had he stayed put he would have caught it with ease. A few minutes later Boag had a shot stopped by Storrier but latched onto the rebound and shot into the right-hand corner. Derby scored a third goal soon after half-time, when Richards collected the ball, made an opening for himself and fired the ball beyond Sutcliffe, this time leaving him no chance of making a save.

Davis of Derby County receiving medical attention following an injury sustained during the game.

This is the Millwall Athletic team that reached the semi-finals. From left to right, back row: R. Hunter, J. Almond, Mr Beveridge, Mr W. Dickinson, W. Phillips, Mr Thorne. Third row: Mr G.A. Saunders, J. Devine, J. Riley, D. Storrier, J. Bell, J.W. Sutcliffe, T. Lee, G. Morris, E. Moor. Second row: A. Easton, H. Astley, B. Hulse, E. Watkins, G. Eccles. Front row: M. Moran, R. Jones. At the end of the 1902/03 season, Millwall finished in seventh place in the Southern League with 14 wins, 3 draws and 13 defeats, scoring a total of 52 goals and conceding 37. Ben Hulse top scored with 14.

Yorkshireman John Sutcliffe became the first Millwall goalkeeper to represent England, playing against Wales at Portsmouth in March 1903. Sutcliffe was one of a rare breed in that he was also selected for England at Rugby Union and had played against the New Zealand touring party. Sutcliffe only spent one season in London, finding the Isle of Dogs uncongenial he moved back to the North and joined Manchester United.

B. Hulse

OGDEN'S CIGARETTES

Liverpool-born Ben Hulse was Millwall's captain for the 1903 semi-final team at Villa Park, having migrated south from New Brighton Tower when they folded. A goal-scoring centre forward, Ben plied his trade in North Greenwich for three seasons, scoring 35 goals in 60 Southern League games, before transferring to Brighton & Hove Albion in 1904.

A sketch of the North Greenwich ground, home of Millwall Athletic from 1901 until 1910. This view looks towards the Manchester Road/Cubitt Town area and the match taking place is supposedly the cup tie versus Middlesbrough in February 1904. The ground, which came to be known as the North Greenwich enclosure, was situated along the East ferry Road, quite near to the old 'Lord Nelson' ground and had to be hastily erected during the summer of 1901 when volunteer labour, along with the new players, all pitched in under the guidance of Elijah Moor to get it prepared for the new season. This hadn't seemed likely a few months previously when the extension of the timber yards had forced the closure of the Dockers' old ground – nearly putting the club out of business. The plan was to accommodate 20,000 spectators with a future development allowing a crowd of 32,000 to be catered for. There was no way the club officials could gauge the capacity of the new ground; in any case the theoretical upper limit of 20,000 was never reached and the largest crowd recorded was when 16,285 turned up to witness Millwall beat Woolwich Arsenal in an FA Cup second round replay on 10 February 1909.

This is the 'Toy Train' – this mode of transport would convey the supporters to the games, and was generally overcrowded on matchdays, hence its name.

The Star Cup was sponsored by the *London Star* newspaper, who during the course of the season would designate certain fixtures involving London clubs, for which points would be awarded to the teams on a result and possibly performance-related basis. The club with the most points at the end of the campaign would then be awarded the trophy. Millwall claimed it in 1908 and it is still in the possession of one of the club's directors to this day.

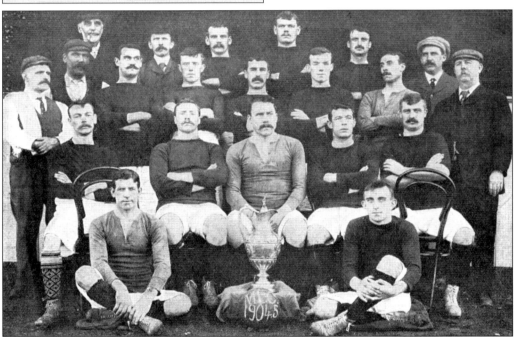

Millwall Athletic, 1904/05. From left to right, back row: W. Dickenson (director), J. Beveridge (secretary), R. McLaren, J.W. Joyce, G. Stevenson, T. Thorne (director). Third row: R. Hunter (trainer), E. Moor (groundsman), F. Baker, R. McLean, J. McLean (captain), J. Blythe, T. Barlow, G.A. Saunders (director). Second row: J. Bradbury, W. Maxwell, J. Calvey, R. Jones, A.E. Watkins. Front row: J. Graham, W. Hunter. Millwall finished fifteenth in the Southern League, winning 11, drawing 7 and losing 16, scoring 38 and conceding 47 goals. Willie Maxwell top scored with 11.

Albert Sutherland, like many Millwall players of his generation, was born and bred on the Isle of Dogs. His number of appearances for his local club was curtailed by the form of regular full-backs Easton and Storrier. Albert had a two-year spell with Woolwich Arsenal before returning to Millwall in 1907. This fine study of the player was captured by local photographer W. Whiffen.

Music to watch games go by – an early form of pre-match entertainment for an encounter against Southampton in 1905.

This is the Millwall Athletic team that took part in the 1905/06 season. From left to right, back row: J. Kifford, J. Joyce, R. Campbell, G. Stevenson, E. Moor, Mr F.G. Weedon. Third row: Mr T. Thorne, R. Hunter, G. Comrie, J. McLean, J. Blythe, G. Marshall, J. Ward, Mr J. Beveridge, Mr G.A. Saunders. Second row: W. Hunter, J. Bradbury, J.A. Twigg, J.B. Millar, A.E. Watkins. Front row: P. Milson, S. Heaton, R. Jones. Millwall finished twelfth in the Southern League, winning 11, drawing 11 and losing 12, scoring 38 and conceding 41 goals. Percy Milson top scored with 13.

This photograph from around 1905 shows the Dockland Settlement. To the left is the entrance to the North Greenwich enclosure, which lay behind an unseen railway viaduct at the rear of the building.

The famous music hall artiste and comedian George Robey was an avid fan of football who would appear in charity games. He is seen here signing registration forms for Millwall with club chairman John Skeggs. George played three Western League games for the Dockers.

Millwall Athletic, 1907/08 season. From left to right, back row: Mr J. Beveridge (secretary), F.D. Shreeve, J. Joyce, A. Sutherland, J. McKenzie. Third row: R. Hunter (trainer), S. Frost, G. Comrie, J. Riley, J. Blythe, Mr W. Dickinson, E. Moor (groundsman). Second row: Mr G.A. Saunders, H. Shand, P. Milson, J.A. Twigg, J. Johnson, W.B. Hunter, Mr T. Thorne. Front row: D. Cunliffe, G. Stevenson (captain), R. Jones. This side finished third in the Southern League. They won 19, drew 8 and lost 11 of their 38 games, scoring 49 goals and conceding 32.

THE FOOTBALL ASSOCIATION, LIMITED.

WEST HAM UNITED *v.* MILLWALL.

PLAYED AT UPTON PARK ON THE 17TH SEPTEMBER, 1906.

REPORT OF COMMISSION :—Messrs. C. W. Alcock, Captain E. G. Curtis and H. Porter.

The Commission having taken evidence are satisfied that the game was not contested in a friendly spirit, the play, on the whole, was far too vigorous, and there were many fouls which were unchecked.

The Match was not properly controlled by Mr. E. Case (Cheshire F.A.) the Referee.

They suspend Jarvis (West Ham United) for 14 days from the 30th October, for what they consider was a serious foul against Dean (Millwall). In imposing this penalty the Commission have had regard to the Player's previous good character.

The players of both teams are censured and warned as to their future conduct.

They suspend Mr. Case from again acting as a Referee during the present season.

With regard to the behaviour of the spectators the Commission are satisfied that there were unseemly incidents, but that these were not sufficiently serious to warrant them taking any other action than requiring the West Ham Club to post special notices on their ground warning their spectators of the consequences which may result from misbehaviour.

The Clubs, having admitted their knowledge of the vigorous and foul play, and that the game was not controlled by the Referee (one of the Clubs having protested to the Western League against Mr. Case again being appointed by the League in any of their future Matches) are severely censured for not having reported the matters to The Football Association.

With regard to the conformation of the Ground.—The Commission decided to recommend to the Council :—

That there should be a clear space of 10 feet between the touch lines and the fence and the supports.

That sheet iron advertisements shall not be attached to the fence unless the edges are protected.

That there should be a clear space of 15 feet between the goal-posts and the spectators.

A misconduct report of the West Ham United *v.* Millwall match, which appears to have been a lively affair (Jarvis had been a Millwall player before joining the Hammers, and was probably trying to prove a point).

Millwall Athletic pictured with the Western League Cup and Star Cup, 1908/09 season. From left to right, back row: R. Hunter (trainer), Mr J. Beveridge (secretary), S. Frost, A. Archer, J. Joyce, H. Carmichael, J. Jeffrey, A. Sutherland, E. Moor (groundsman), Mr W. Dickinson (director). Middle row: Mr G.A. Saunders (director), H. Shand, D. Cunliffe, J. Blythe, G. Comrie, J. Riley, R. Jones, J. Tellum. Front row: A. Dean, F. Vincent, G. Stevenson, A. Twigg, W.B. Hunter. Having finished in third place the previous season, this campaign was something of an anti-climax as Millwall finished eleventh in the Southern League, winning 16, drawing 6 and losing 18 of their games, scoring 59 and conceding 61 goals. However, it wasn't all doom and gloom, as what would be the last Western League championship was retained and another piece of silverware, the London Challenge Cup, was won. This was achieved with victories over Ilford (6-0), Chelsea (2-1) and Tottenham (2-0 in the semi-final at West Ham) before Millwall vanquished Leyton 2-0 in the final (again at the Hammers' ground) with two Alf Twigg goals securing the trophy. One of the players performing heroics at this time was John 'Tiny' Joyce, who was regarded as being something of a giant, standing at over six feet tall and weighing in at around fourteen stone – his goal kicks would often reach from one penalty area to the other. Tiny's career would stretch to 385 games and his association with Millwall continued until 1933, as he held the post of assistant trainer and then assistant groundsman. Dick Jones was another player of this period who was with Millwall as long as Joyce. Although English by birth, Jones was a Welsh international who was capped twice in 1906. Brought up on the island, Dick was a product of the Millwall St Johns club and was no doubt introduced to the game by his elder brothers Eddie (who was known as 'Taff') and Willie (see page 23) who had played for Millwall Athletic in the 1890s. Dick's partner on the left flank of the Millwall attack was Billy Hunter – another of the many Scots who had migrated south during the tenure of fellow Scot and namesake Bob Hunter. Bill would give the Dockers five years of loyal service in which he would appear in 224 games and score 69 goals.

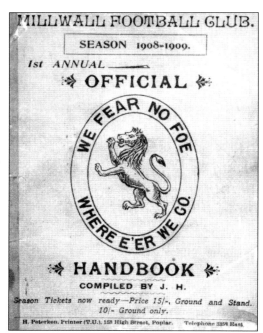

The cover from Millwall's first handbook, with a motto which had been translated from Scots-Gaelic into English.

The front (left) and reverse (right) of the London Challenge Cup winners medal of 1908/09. This particular gong was awarded to Jim Jeffrey. Jim was one of the many Scots who came south to join Millwall, which he did in the summer of 1908 from Dundee. Jim was a sturdy full-back and would spend the rest of his career with Millwall, for whom he played 226 games before retiring just before the First World War. In his five seasons with the club he missed just eleven games and on one occasion he was selected for an England trial match before it was realised that he had been born in Perthshire!

Caygill's 'Krect Card, the forerunner of today's match programme, was printed on the morning of the game – which went a long way to justify the title – and was sold for 1d. The front cover (above left) and teamsheet (above right) shown here come from the issue for the home game against Bristol Rovers on 12 October 1912. Millwall won the match 6-0.

The Western League Challenge Cup, which Millwall had won in 1907/08 and won again in 1908/09. The club's success in the 1908/09 competition came through winning a twelve team league, which included the likes of West Ham, Portsmouth, Southampton and Brentford. After finishing top of Section B, Millwall were pitched against Section A champions Brighton & Hove Albion. The final was held at West Ham's Boleyn Ground and ended in a 1-1 draw, Alf Twigg scoring the Millwall goal. The replay took place at the same venue nearly three weeks later on 22 April 1909 and it was Twigg again and Dan Cunliffe who scored the goals to give Millwall a 2-1 victory and the trophy.

Island resident J.G. Hames was a prolific writer of verse in his day, often describing Millwall's exploits. This poem is one of many he penned that was published in the local press. Hames was also a Freeman of the City of London.

Photo by Brunton, Burnley.

Lancashire-born General Stevenson joined Millwall in May 1903 from Wellingborough (having already had spells with Liverpool and Barnsley) and made his debut against West Ham United in September of that year. Stevenson, who at 5ft $7\frac{1}{2}$ in and 12 stone was a sturdy and ferocious tackler, became a firm favourite with the fans and a mark of his consistency is that he is just one of five players to appear in over 200 Southern League matches. A typical full-back of the period, he was selected for the South *v*. North England trial games in 1904 and 1905, but unfortunately did not win a full cap. After appearing in 318 games for Athletic, in which he scored 9 goals, he returned to his native county. *Above:* Stevenson's loyalty to Millwall was rewarded with a benefit match against Portsmouth in 1909, which the Dockers won 1-0. *Right:* A cigarette card depicting the loyal Lancastrian.

Millwall Athletic pictured with the London FA Cup and the Western League Cup, 1909/10. From left to right, back row: Mr J. Beveridge (secretary), A. Archer, W. Waller, J. Joyce, H. Carmichael, J. Atkinson, J. Jeffrey. Middle row: F. Vincent, S. Frost, J. Martin, A. McCormack, J. Wilson, J. Blythe, D. Glen, A. Twigg. Front row: A Garrett, J. Morris, G. Stevenson, R. Jones, W. Semple. Millwall finished in sixteenth position in the Southern League, having won 15, drawn 7 and lost 20 games, scoring 45 and conceding 59 goals. John Martin was the top scorer with 12.

Joseph Hawkins was born at Millwall in 1889 and signed as a professional during the 1910/11 season. A tall half-back, he would make just three appearances in his time at the club, mainly because of the presence of Joe Wilson, Sammy Frost and Billy Voisey, who were holding down regular places in the side. Joe was a member of the Poplar and Blackwall Rowing Club and in later life was a chief tally clerk with a firm of stevedores. A local man with a local job, Joe resided in the West Ferry Road. He is pictured here with his fiancee Susan – who was a lifelong supporter of the team, going all over the country to watch them play – in 1909.

Two
South of the River
1910-1920

Millwall Athletic, 1910/11. From left to right, back row: Mr W. Dickenson (director), A. Hunter, J. Hawkins, A. Rice, J. Atkinson, H. Carmichael, J. Jeffrey, R. Payne, W. Voisey, E. Moor, Mr Beveridge, Mr F.G. Weedon. Middle row: J. Harrower, A. Garrett, S. Frost, J. Wilson, J. Blythe, A. Taylor, S. Wayment, C. Elliot, Mr Thorne. Front row: J. Morris, J. Martin, R. Walker, W. Martin, J. Smith, F. Vincent, H.B. Lipsham. Millwall finished in fifteenth position in the Southern League, having won 11, drawn 9 and lost 18, scoring 42 and conceding 54 goals. John Martin top scored again with 12.

An artist's impression of Cold Blow Farm before Elijah Moor and friends got their hands on it, to transform it into the famous Den, that all Millwall supporters came to love and opponents to dread.

When Millwall took over their ground, cows were grazing on it, and it was so rough that they had to hire a steam-roller to level out the deep ruts!

Brighton & Hove Albion were the first visitors to Cold Blow Lane on 22 October 1910. This photograph of the official opening of the ground shows Millwall skipper Joe Wilson talking to the guest of honour Lord Kinnaird. Lord Kinnaird was the President of the Football Association and was given the honour of turning the golden key to open the gate leading from the Pavilion to the playing area. Unfortunately, the historic moment was somewhat spoiled when Brighton scored the only goal of the game to send the crowd of 20,000 home disappointed.

MILLWALL'S NEW GROUND.

After many years sojourn at East Ferry Road and North Greenwich, the old "Lions of the South," Millwall, have migrated to the more populous district of New Cross. The opening ceremony of the new ground was performed on Saturday, the Southern League Champions, Brighton and Hove Albion F.C., providing the successful opposition in a 1-goal match.

EXCLUSIVE PICTURES BY OUR OWN PHOTOGRAPHERS

1. The stand above the dressing-room, with two ringed heads qualifying their owners for a guinea each at our expense.
2. Lord Kinnaird handing the ball to the opposing captains, Leeming, of Brighton (in stripes), and Wilson, of Millwall. To the right of Lord Kinnaird is Mr. Skeggs (one of Millwall's directors) and the referee, Mr. W. J. Heath.
3. Carmichael, the Millwall goal keeper.
4. Lord Kinnaird declares the ground open.
5. Mr. G. A. Saunders, holding a gold model of a lion, the club's emblem, in his right hand.
6. E. Moor, the Millwall groundsman.
7. The band of the Dr. Barnardo's Boys Home, which has ever received strong support from the Millwall club.
8. A corner of the ground, showing the tremendous crowd which attended the new field.
9. A sidelight of the game—Millwall repelling an attack.

Look out for our special photographers at ALL sporting gatherings.

The report on the opening day at The Den from *Lotinga's Weekly* of 29 October 1910.

OFFICIAL PROGRAMME

& RECORD OF THE CLUB.

MILLWALL F. C.

ISSUED EVERY MATCH DAY. PRICE ONE PENNY.

OCTOBER 22ND, 1910.

THE NEW CROSS EMPIRE,

NEW CROSS ROAD, S.E.

6.40   **TWICE NIGHTLY**   9.0

MISS HETTY KING
The Popular Male Impersonator.

LEE & KINGSTON
In a Musical Absurdity.

FERRY CORWAY
The Unique Musical Clown.

PARK'S ETON BOYS
give several good songs.

LA SUPERBE
In Modern Dances.

BURLEY & BURLEY
Acrobatic Comedians.

HARRY MAY HEMSLEY
Impersonator.

MISS MARQUIS
and her Wonderful Stud of Trained Ponies.

ADELE MORAN
The Great International Comedienne.

Next Week : Triumphant Return of . **LA MILO,** The Inimitable .. Breathing Marble

AND A GRAND LONDON STAR COMPANY.

H. PRYCE & SON, The Woolwich Printers (T.U. Federation), 31, 33 & 35 Powis Street, Woolwich.

The front cover of the match programme for the first ever game at The Den.

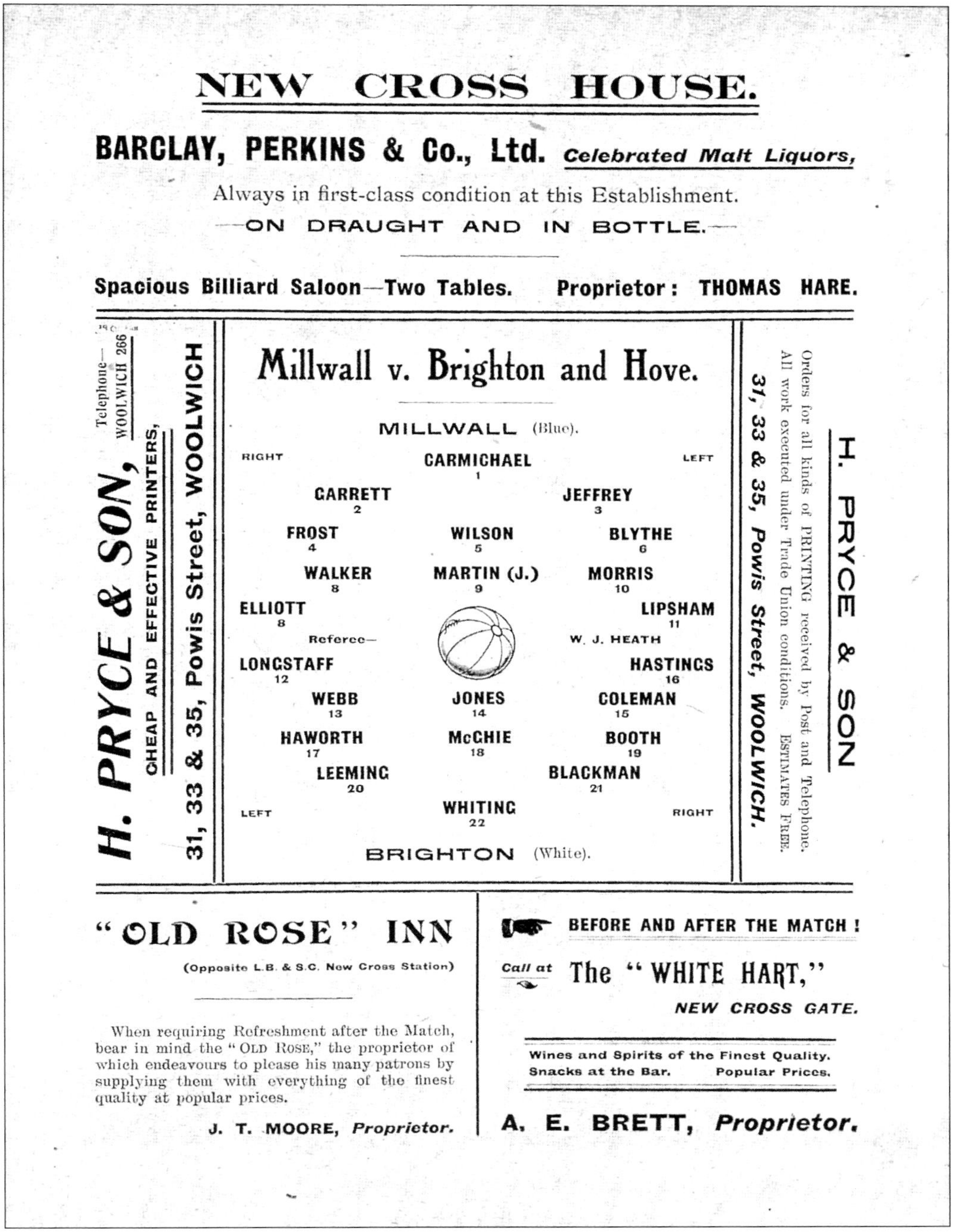

Millwall v. Brighton and Hove.

MILLWALL (Blue).

RIGHT   CARMICHAEL   LEFT
1

GARRETT   JEFFREY
2   3

FROST   WILSON   BLYTHE
4   5   6

WALKER   MARTIN (J.)   MORRIS
8   9   10

ELLIOTT   LIPSHAM
8   11

Referee—   W. J. HEATH

LONGSTAFF   HASTINGS
12   16

WEBB   JONES   COLEMAN
13   14   15

HAWORTH   McCHIE   BOOTH
17   18   19

LEEMING   BLACKMAN
20   21

LEFT   WHITING   RIGHT
22

BRIGHTON (White).

The teamsheet from that historic occasion.

MILLWALL PLAYERS WHO REPRESENTED THE SOUTHERN LEAGUE

(INTER-LEAGUE)

J. WILSON
1910

H. LIPSHAM
1910-11

J. JEFFREY
1911

S. FROST
1911

W. DAVIS
1912-14

R. LIDDELL
1914

J. KIRKWOOD
1914

H. B. MOODY
1914

A collage made up from rare Taddy cigarette cards featuring some of the Millwall stars of the period, including Bert Lipsham. Bert had given Sheffield United many years of splendid service and gained several honours, including two FA Cup final appearances, an England cap in 1902 and two appearances for the Football League against the Irish League. Moving to Fulham in 1908, where he played 56 times in the Second Division, he came to Millwall as a player in 1910 and was appointed player-manager in May 1911. The team's form improved straightaway the following term – in which he signed the player who would become one of Millwall's greatest goalscorers, Welshman Wally Davies. Bert carried on his managerial career throughout the First World War. He left The Den in the early 1920s to take up an appointment at West Norwood before moving on to Northfleet. Bert emigrated to Canada in 1923 and helped to establish the game in that country. He passed away in 1932.

SOUTHERN LEAGUERS' TRIUMPH.

The new ground of the Millwall F.C. at New Cross has been very much in the public eye since Lord Kinnaird performed the opening ceremony there. It is probable, however, that it will know no bigger contest this season than the meeting of picked teams representing the Southern League and Scottish League last Monday week. This game was watched with much care by members of the international selection committees of both countries. The Southern Leaguers confirmed their earlier victory over a combined Football League XI. by a well-earned 1-0 success.

1. The inscription on the grand stand at New Cross.
2. The winning Southern League team: Back row (left to right): Bamlett (referee), Maley (linesman), Brittan (Northampton), Kitchen (West Ham), Walker (Swindon), Booth (Brighton & Hove), Crisp (linesman). Front row: Jefferson (Swindon), Fleming (Swindon), Reid (Brentford), Wilson (Millwall), Trueman (Southampton), Moody (Luton), Barnes (Queen's Park Rangers), Bob Hunter (Millwall's trainer-manager).
3. Brownlie of the Third Lanark, the Scottish goalkeeper, taking things easily.
4. The toss-up between (to the left) Jimmy Hay, of the Celtic, and (to the right) J. Wilson, of Millwall, with the referee, Mr. H. S. Bamlett, in the centre.

5. Members of the crowd watching the game, with two "marked men" due to receive honorariums of a guinea each.
6. The Scottish League XI.: Back row (left to right): W. Maley (Celtic), J. Quinn (Celtic), T. Collins (Heart of Midlothian), J. Mitchell (Kilmarnock), J. Brownlie (Third Lanark), W. Ward (vice-president, Partick Thistle), J. Young (Celtic), W. MacAndrew (Secretary), J. Hendry (Rangers), H. S. Bamlett (referee). Front row: R. Walker (Heart of Midlothian), W. J. Reilchan (Celtic), J. Simpson (Falkirk), J. Hay (Celtic, captain), H. C. Dainty (Dundee), A. Bennett (Rangers), R. Templeton (Kilmarnock), Minnie (Falkirk, trainer).
7. The Scottish goalkeeper's best save with the left hand—among many very good ones.

Joe Wilson was a fine captain of Millwall and he had the honour of leading the Southern League against their Scottish counterparts at The Den on 24 October 1910; this report comes from *Lotinga's Weekly* of 5 November 1910. Wilson was another in the long line of Millwall players to originate from Lancashire. An experienced centre-back, he had begun his career with local clubs Wigan Athletic, Darwen and Blackburn Rovers, before transferring south to Brighton & Hove Albion in 1904. After five seasons on the South Coast, he joined Millwall for the last full season on the Island. A great leader, he exercised splendid judgement, and whilst at Millwall won two Kent Senior Shield medals, in 1913 and 1914, plus one for winning the London Challenge Cup in 1915 when the Lions defeated Arsenal 2-1. Joe created a record that will never be broken when he played in 121 consecutive Southern League games. Surviving the First World War, he played one more season for the Lions before returning to Lancashire to play for Rochdale.

Annual Report, 1910-11.

The Directors submit their Report for the year ended 30th April, 1911.

The most important happening of the season was the opening of the new ground at New Cross, which event took place on the 22nd October, 1910, when the Club was honoured by the presence of the popular President of the Football Association, the Right Hon. Lord Kinnaird, who in a few well chosen words expressed his conviction that all Football enthusiasts would be unanimous in complimenting Millwall on the possession of such a home, and wishing the Club every success in the future. The very large number attending the opening match are not likely to forget the scene of enthusiasm, and our old friends from Brighton will always remember that they had the pleasure of winning the first match played on the new ground.

That the removal from the Isle of Dogs was a wise step was immediately proved by the attendances at the opening match and on the following Monday, when the first Inter-League Match between the Scottish and the Southern Leagues was played. The ground was also selected by the Football Association as the venue for the Inter-national match with Wales, which was duly played on the 13th March, 1911, in the presence of what is believed to be a record crowd for a midweek Inter-national match. The choice of the new ground for these important fixtures was much appreciated.

The actual cost of laying out the ground is not yet ascertained, but it will be approximately £10,000, and the Architect, Mr. A. Leitch, and the Contractors, Messrs. Humphreys, of Knightsbridge, fully deserved all the complimentary expressions which were made by the many prominent men in the Football world who were present at the opening matches.

The receipts during the year amounted to £7,772 7s. 1d., as compared with £3,881 0s. 8d. of the year 1909-10, and the expenditure to £7,459 8s. 8d., as compared with £3,999 18s. 9d. It will be noticed that the expenditure includes £1,122 19s. 0d. on account of cost of laying out the ground.

From a playing point of view the first team was not so successful as was to be hoped in the first season at New Cross, and towards the end of April there was considerable anxiety as to the possibility of relegation to the Second Division of the Southern League, which fate was ultimately avoided, the Club finishing fifteenth in the table.

The Reserve team had a most successful season in the Kent and London Leagues. In the Kent League the team tied with the Crystal Palace Reserves for top place, and in a deciding match played on the ground of the Woolwich Arsenal Club had the satisfaction of winning the Championship. In the London League they were top of their Division, a position obtained by Queen's Park Rangers in their Division. The match to determine the Championship of this League was won by Millwall by 3—0, and the Millwall Reserves are to be congratulated on becoming holders of the trophies of both Leagues in which they competed.

The details of the Competition Matches played are :—

	Played.	Won.	Lost.	Drawn.	Goals. For	Against.
Southern League	38	11	18	9	46	55
London League	15	12	3	0	42	14
Kent League	27	21	4	2	73	24
F.A. Cup	1	0	1	0	1	2
London Senior Cup	3	2	1	0	3	3
London Charity Competition	1	0	1	0	0	3

The Directors retiring are Messrs. J. B. Skeggs, T. Thorne and G. A. Saunders, who offer themselves for re-election.

J. B. SKEGGS,
Chairman.

The Annual Report that was issued at the end of the 1910/11 season, which shows an

The Millwall Football and Athletic Company, Ltd.

PROFIT AND LOSS ACCOUNT,

For the period from 1st May, 1910, to 30th April, 1911.

Dr.		£ s. d.	£ s. d.	Cr.		£ s. d.	£ s. d.
To Players' Wages, Expenses and Transfers	... ...		3459 6 11	By Gate Receipts			6719 9 7
„ Guarantees, etc., to Visiting Teams ...	... ...		971 12 5	„ Receipts from Shoot			461 19 0
„ Payments to Humphrey's, Limited ...	... ...		969 3 2	„ Guarantees—Away Matches			455 7 1
„ Rent, Rates and Taxes	... ...		457 5 1	„ Programmes			70 19 11
„ Match Expenses	... ...		380 11 11	„ Season Tickets...			35 1 6
„ Trainer's and Groundsmen's Wages...	... ...		203 10 0	„ Rents Receivable			29 10 0
„ Rail and Travelling Expenses	... ...		191 14 11				
„ Printing and Advertising ...	... ...		184 9 0				
„ Refreshments. Teas, etc. ...	... ...		154 18 10				
„ Interest to Humphrey's, Limited	... ...		136 18 4				
„ Secretarial Expenses	... ...		78 11 0				
„ Upkeep of Ground	... ...		76 19 2				
„ Poplar Hospital	18 12 2						
„ Seamen's Hospital	18 12 1						
„ Bolton Colliery Fund	10 3 2						
„ Reading Football Club	10 0 0						
„ Deptford Invicta Football Club ...	2 2 0						
„ Kennedy Fund...	1 1 0						
		60 10 5					
„ Legal Expenses	... ...	44 12 0					
„ Subscriptions, etc., to Leagues ...	... ...	33 19 6					
„ Interest on Debentures	... ...	25 17 6					
„ Postages, Telegrams and Stationery...	... ...	23 9 9					
„ Bank Charges	... ...	12 4 1					
„ National Telephone Co.	... ...	11 5 6					
„ Sundries	... ...	6 9 2					
„ Balance carried down	... ...	312 18 5					
			£7772 7 1				£7772 7 1
To Millwall Ground Account written off	...	£1017 15 5		By Balance brought down			£312 18 5
				„ „ as per last Balance Sheet			625 17 8
				„ „ carried to Balance Sheet			78 19 4
			£1017 15 5				£1017 15 5

BALANCE SHEET,

As at 30th April, 1911.

LIABILITIES.		£ s. d.	£ s. d.	ASSETS.		£ s. d.
Capital Authorised			1000 0 0	Lease, Buildings, Fixtures, etc.		
Issued—				Monies expended at "The Den" to date ...		7614 1 7
In fully paid Shares, 500 of £1 each	500 0 0			London County and Westminster Bank.		
321 Shares of £1, fully called up...	321 0 0			Cash Bank at Millwall Branch		74 11 11
		821 0 0		Profit and Loss Account.		
Less, Calls in arrears		66 0 0		Balance as per Balance Sheet		78 19 4
			755 0 0	Sundry Debtors		3 3 0
Debentures—						
Issue of 98 Debentures of £10 each			980 0 0			
Sundry Creditors—						
Humphrey's, Limited, on Certificates issued to date	5305 5 2					
Tradesmen, Secretarial, etc.... ...	715 17 5					
Petty Cash Account	14 13 3		6035 15 10			
			£7770 15 10			£7770 15 10

improvement in the financial situation since moving south of the river.

England played Wales at The Den on 13 March 1911. This was the only full international ever to be held there and was watched by a crowd of 25,000 (at the time a record for a England mid-week fixture). England won the match 3-1. A contemporary report of the time commented that 'The match was a remarkable one in many respects. The English side, who won in the end so easily, failed to gain any advantage when playing with a strong wind behind them, for although they had much of the better of the football the Welsh defence was very sound. The game had lasted for over an hour before there was any scoring, the home side showed to the most advantage when the wind beat in their faces and the sleet and snow had made the turf slippery. Considering the conditions during the second half the play of the English side reached a high standard, and when once they had scored they soon put the result beyond doubt. England had made three alterations in the team that did so moderately against Ireland, bringing in three amateurs – the Rev. K.R.G. Hunt, V.J. Woodward and G.W. Webb – and these changes made all the difference to the side. Hunt and Warren were in a higher class than Wedlock, their partner in the half-back line, and Woodward was the best of the forwards. Woodward was in fine form and he and Evans made the left wing the most effective attacking force in the match. He scored two of the goals by neatly heading through two centres by Simpson, who would certainly have been more prominent had he been better served by Fleming. Crompton was in good form at the back, although he was occasionally at fault in kicking, and Pennington got through a great deal of useful work. The Welsh inside forwards never settled down to an effective game, owing to the good spoiling tactics of the English backs'. *Above*: Action from the match as England pile on the pressure in the Welsh penalty area.

The England and Wales Association International

Which was played in alternating outbursts of snow and wind on the Millwall club's new ground at New Cross.

1. The Welshmen kick-off.
2. Wales coming on to the field, with the crack outside-right, Billy Meredith, just coming through the gateway.
3. The English team make their appearance, Vivian Woodward being followed by Ben Warren and the new centre-forward, G. W. Webb, the dashing West Ham United amateur.
4. Woodward wins the toss-up.
5. Some of the crowd with two of its members "ringed-out" to receive our award of a guinea apiece.
6. The English captain (Woodward) heads the third and final goal from a centre of Simpson's.
7. Webb scores England's second goal with a hot drive just under the cross-bar.
8. The popular secretary and guiding spirit of the Football Association, Mr. F. J. Wall, a leading figure always at the bigger games.
9. The Welsh goalkeeper fists away a dropping ball as Webb comes along to try and get his head to it.

"Lotinga's Weekly" Speciality—Lifelike Pictures by Land and Water.

The *Lotinga's Weekly* pictorial summary of the game.

Millwall Athletic with the Southern League Shield, 1911/12. From left to right, back row: R. Hunter, Mr W. Dickinson, Mr J. Beveridge, J. Hawkins, A. Brown, F.R. Wood, Mr F. Weedon, J. Kirkwood, W. Voisey, R. Jones, E. Moor, A. Lipsham. Middle row: Mr G.A. Saunders, A. Carvossa, F. Vincent, S. Frost, J. Wilson, J. Borthwick, R. Liddell, W. Martin, W. Davies, Mr T. Thorne. Front row: S. Wayment, J. Morris, F. Wilding, J. Smith, J. Jeffrey, T. Quinn, A.E. Taylor, C. Elliot, J. Kenyon. Millwall finished the season in eighth position in Southern League with 15 wins, 10 draws and 13 defeats, scoring 60 goals and conceding 57. Joint top-scorers for the club were Joe Wilson and Wally Davies with 12 each.

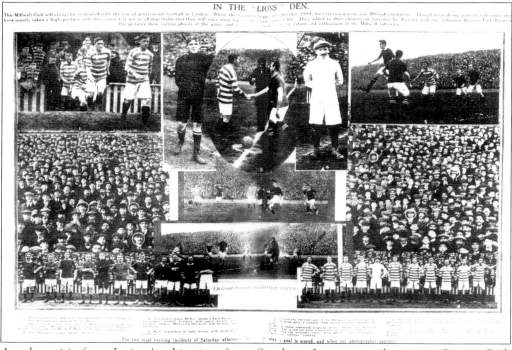

Another visit from *Lotinga's*, this time for a Southern League match against Queens Park Rangers on 21 October 1911. Note that those spectators fortunate enough to their head ringed in the photograph won a dollar (25p).

The Millwall players going through their paces in a training session in September 1911.

Millwall Athletic with the Southern League Shield, 1912/13. From left to right, back row: A. Gillies, E. Hegazi, R. Jones. Third row: W. Dickenson, R. Hunter (trainer), S. Frost, J. Hawkins, A. Brown, M. Spendiff, H. Taylor, J. Kirkwood, J. Jamieson, S. Wayment, E. Moor (groundsman), B. Lipsham (manager), J. Beveridge. Second row: G.A. Saunders (director), J. Kenyon, W. Voisey, J. Borthwick, A. Jeffrey, J. Wilson, R. Liddell, W. Martin, A.E. Taylor, T. Thorne (director). Front row: R.J. Dilley, F. Vincent, E. Brown, T. Quinn, W. Davis, H. Moody, C. Elliott, W. Grumbridge. Millwall finished in sixth position in the Southern League, having won 19, drawn 7 and lost 12 games, scoring 62 and conceding 43 goals. The top scorer was Wally Davies with 23. This team group photograph includes Hegazi, an Egyptian national who played twice for Millwall and who became a Cambridge 'Blue' in 1914 when the university beat their Oxford rivals 2-1. A student at St Catherine's College, Hegazi would also assist Fulham and Dulwich Hamlet whilst studying in England. Sammy 'Snowball' Frost, the first Millwall-born player to win an FA Cup winners medal, is also in the photograph: he achieved this in 1904 with Manchester City, but after a footballing scandal in the north, as a result of which he and his City team-mates were suspended, he returned to Millwall to see out the rest of his injury-cursed career. After retiring, Sammy took a confectionary shop in Grundy Street Poplar, but misfortune seemed to follow him around and in 1926 he committed suicide. Some of Snowball's colleagues pictured here were also born on the 'Island', including Billy Voisey (a highly decorated combatant in the First World War), goal-scorer 'Buck' Vincent, Joe Hawkins and the much-travelled Billy Martin – who after initially appearing for Millwall in the early 1900s came back to his home-town club after plying his trade in the north of England with clubs like Oldham, Leeds City and Stockport. Another striker was Luton-born Bert Moody, who would still be turning out for the team at the age of forty. The club secretary at the time was Scotsman John Beveridge, who after joining Millwall Athletic in 1894 would go on to serve the club for over fifty years.

SOUTHERN LEAGUE CLUBS.

Our photographers visit Park Royal and the "Den."

EXCLUSIVE PICTURES FROM OUR OWN PHOTOGRAPHERS

The Rangers do a sprint for the benefit of the Lotinga Camera

"The Rangers"

"Catch Ball" A fine thing for quickening the eye.

Getting fit

Millwall. F.C.

James Cowan, the popular Manager of the Rangers

It is most appropriate that Queen's Park Rangers (last year's champions) should be amongst the first of the Southern League clubs to engage our attention. They have gathered together a most capable side, and their doings this season will be closely followed in our pages. Millwall, the winners of the League in the first years of its existence, also promise to give a good account of themselves, both in League and Cup fixtures.

Lotinga's held high hopes for the chances of Millwall Football Club in the pending season.

63

SATURDAY'S SPORTOGRAPHS.

"Weather foul or weather fair—'Lotinga's' cameras always there."

Pictures of the S.C.C.U. Cycle Championship Meeting, at Herne Hill track; and Millwall's opening practice match at the "Den." Further pictures of these events will be published in our next issue.

It's the start of the 1912/13 season, and the traditional Blues versus Whites public trial match was held in August. All the monies received from these games would be donated to the various local hospitals and charities.

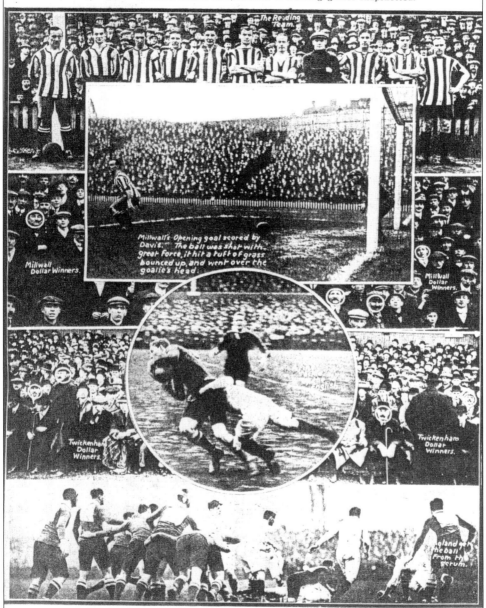

SATURDAY'S SOCCER AND RUGGER.

The England v. Soutn Africa and Millwall v. Reading games snapshotted.

The Reading Team.

Millwall's Opening goal scored by Davis. The ball was shot with great force, it hit a tuft of grass, bounced up, and went over the goalie's head.

Millwall Dollar Winners.

Millwall Dollar Winners.

Twickenham Dollar Winners.

Twickenham Dollar Winners.

The event of the season for Rugby enthusiasts was the South Africans' fixture with England, and which, after months of discussion, ended in the Colonials' favour, so that the visitors have thus won all their Internationals, and earned the admiration of all Rugger followers. At Soccer, Millwall, in an intensely interesting game, just managed to beat Reading, thereby elating the Lions' supporters.

Again next week will a few of the jockeys' and champions' anecdotes appear in these rages.

Millwall opened the New Year of 1913 by shading a seven goal thriller against Reading. Note that the train in the upper central picture had stopped to watch the game.

THE DEN: "LIONS" v. MIDDLESBROUGH.

Where the home team played well but could not score.

Dollar & Double Dollar Winners

Mending the Net after a hot shot from the Millwall attack.

Williamson (Middlesbrough's goalie) saves a good shot.

The Captains toss up

More Dollar & Double Dollar winners.

e Cup tie fight between Millwall (Southern League) and Middlesbrough (First Division) was regarded
many as London's tit-bit, and so it proved. Aft r a great struggle the result was a no-score draw,
t the Northerners will probably win the replay. It is noticeable that "Lotinga's Weekly" was in
evidence among the onlookers, and more pictures of the crowd will be published next week.

E NEXT WEEK'S ISSUE OF "LOTINGA'S."

Lotinga's Weekly were frequent visitors to The Den and this montage of photographs was taken from the issue of 18 January 1913 and shows the Millwall *v.* Middlesbrough FA Cup tie from the weekend before. The paper reported that 'The Cup tie fight between Millwall (Southern League) and Middlesbrough (First Division) was regarded by many as London's tit-bit, and so it proved. After a great struggle the result was a no-score draw, but the Northerners will probably win the replay.'

As a new stadium The Den was very much in demand. On 3 March 1913 the ground hosted a representative match between the London League and the Paris League.

The opposing captains at the toss-up for the London League *v.* Paris League match.

This share certificate was issued to director Tom Thorne's son, Dennis, on his birth in 1913. Tom became chairman during the 1915/16 season. Dennis is now living in Australia.

Millwall Football Club, 1913/14. From left to right, back row: J. Kirkwood, P. Warren, H. Taylor, A. Pratt, W. Woodley, R. Jones, A. Gillies. Third row: W. Dickinson (director), R. Hunter (trainer), F.G. Weedon (director), W. Voisey, J. Hawkins, A. Garrett, A. Taylor, E. Moor (groundsman), J.B. Skeggs (director), H.B. Lipsham (manager). Second row: G.A. Saunders (director), W. Sullivan, H. Butterworth, J. Borthwick, J. Jeffrey, J. Wilson, S. Wayment, R. Liddell, J. Beveridge (secretary), T. Thorne (director). Front row: G. Dodd, R. Dilley, R. Noble, W. Davis, H. Moody, F. Vincent, S. Lamb, G. Porter. Millwall finished the season in fifteenth position in the Southern League, having won 11, drawn 12 and lost 15 of their matches, scoring 51 goals and conceding 56. Wally Davies top scored with 18.

VARIOUS SPORTING VENUES LAST SATURDAY.

T ABLE TO BE PRESENT—*IT IS ALL HERE!*

An early season encounter with Crystal Palace at The Den in September 1913, captured here by *Lotinga's Weekly*.

The two teams pictured for the Southern League *v.* Football League game at The Den on 9 February 1914. The Football League side that won 3-1 was almost identical to the England team that had faced Ireland the week before.

A postcard advertising a cup tie. It has a stamp cancellation date on the reverse side dated April 1914.

Scot Bob Hunter was appointed trainer of the Southern League team which played host to the Scottish League at The Den in February 1914, in which two Millwall men, Wally Davies and Bob Liddell, were chosen for the Southern League. A signing from Custom House in the Autumn of 1911, Wally Davies was a wonderful footballer with great close control skill allied with a fine balance. As such he was one of a dying breed: centre forwards of his type would have been more likely around twenty years or more before his time. The scorer of what the press of the day described as 'a wonder goal' in a cup tie against Bradford City which Millwall won 1-0 in January 1914, Wally was a Welsh international who had been born in Mold in 1888. He had played against England at Ashton Gate where he had scored a goal in Wales' narrow 4-3 defeat. He also represented the Southern League on six occasions. During the First World War he soldiered in Italy where he sustained an ankle injury that finished his playing career. Tragically, he was found drowned in Bow Creek in mysterious circumstances in May 1937. Bob Liddell hailed from the North East and joined Millwall from Newcastle United in June 1911 for £150. Liddell had played in just 14 games in his time at St James' Park, where he understudied the great wing half Peter McWilliam. After joining the Lions he played 117 Southern League and FA Cup fixtures over the next four seasons, also representing the Southern League against the Football League in 1914 and the Football, Scottish and Irish Leagues the following season.

The Millwall squad for the 1914/15 season. Despite the outbreak of the First World War in August, the season was played out in full. However, at the end of the season it was accepted that the war would go on a lot longer than people expected and regular competition was curtailed until the end of hostilities. From left to right, back row: H.B. Lipsham (manager), F.G. Weedon (director), W. Beckerleg, J. Orme, F. O'Hara, S.A. Wayment, A. Gillies, R. Jones, E. Moor. Third row: R. Hunter, W. Dickinson (director), R. Dilley, R. Liddell, J. Borthwick, J. Kirkwood, J. Nuttall, A. Garrett, W. Woodley, R. Peck, J. Beveridge (secretary). Second row: G.A. Saunders (director), R. Noble, H. Butterworth, F. Whittaker, J. Williams, J. Williams, W. Davis, H. Moody, J. Wilson, S. Lamb, J.B. Skeggs (director), T. Thorne (director). Front row: G. Porter, A.E. Miller, J. Fort, F.W. Thompson, W. Nicholl, H. Makepeace. Millwall finished the season in eighth position in the Southern League, winning 16, drawing 10 and losing 12, scoring 50 and conceding 51 goals. Wally Davies was top scorer for the fourth season in a row with 14.

MEN OF MILLWALL

Hundreds of Football enthusiasts are joining the Army daily.

Don't be left behind.

Let the Enemy hear the "LION'S ROAR."

Join and be in at

THE FINAL

and give them a

KICK OFF THE EARTH

Apply:
West Africa House, opposite National Theatre, Kingsway.

This leaflet was distributed on matchdays at The Den during the First World War.

These two memorial plaques were salvaged from The Den by Colin Sayer from underneath the Cold Blow Lane terrace. The first commemorates four fallen Millwall players who died during the Great War, and the other deals with visits by various members of the Royal Family to The Den. Note that the other three ancient monuments are the compilers of this book.

MILLWALL
FOOTBALL CLUB

OFFICIAL PROGRAMME

XMAS DAY, DECEMBER 25TH, 1918.

FIXTURES FOR 1918-19.

Date.	Opponents.	Ground.	Goals For Ag'st	Date.	Opponents.	Ground.	Goals For Ag'st
Sep. 7	Chelsea	Home	1 6	Jan. 4	The Arsenal	Away	
,, 14	The Arsenal	Away	0 4	,, 11	Crystal Palace	Home	
,, 21	Crystal Palace	Home	0 2	,, 18	Queen's Park R.	Away	
,, 28	Queen's Park R'ng'rs	Away	0 1	,, 25	Clapton Orient	Away	
Oct. 5	Clapton Orient	Home	1 0	Feb. 1	Fulham	Home	
,, 12	Fulham	Away	0 1	,, 8	Brentford	Away	
,, 19	Brentford	Away	2 4	,, 15	West Ham United	Home	
,, 26	Tottenham Hotspur	Home	0 2	,, 22	Chelsea	Away	
Nov. 2	Chelsea	Away	1 0	Mar. 1	The Arsenal	Home	
,, 9	The Arsenal	Home	3 3	,, 8	Crystal Palace	Away	
,, 16	Crystal Palace	Away	2 2	,, 15	Queen's Park R.	Home	
,, 23	Queen's Park R'ng'rs	Home	4 1	,, 22	Clapton Orient	Home	
,, 30	Clapton Orient	Home	1 1	,, 29	Fulham	Away	
Dec. 7	Fulham	Away	1 0	Apl. 5	Brentford	Home	
,, 14	Brentford	Home	3 1	,, 12	West Ham United	Away	
,, 21	Tottenham Hotspur	Away	3 0	,, 18	Tottenham Hotspur	Away	
,, 25	West Ham United	Home		,, 19			
,, 26	West Ham United	Away		,, 21	Tottenham Hotspur	Home	
,, 28	Chelsea	Home		,, 26			

LONDON COMBINATION.

	Played	Won	Drn.	Lost	Goals For	Goals Agst.	Pts.
Brentford	16	9	4	3	46	19	22
Chelsea	16	9	3	4	41	20	21
Crystal Palace	16	8	3	5	34	31	19
West Ham United	16	8	2	6	30	22	18
Tottenham Hotspur	16	8	2	6	25	30	18
The Arsenal	16	7	3	6	31	27	17
Fulham	16	6	3	7	33	24	15
Millwall	16	6	3	7	22	28	15
Queen's Pk. Rangers	16	6	2	8	27	35	14
Clapton Orient	16	0	1	15	10	60	1

Next Match at The Den,

CHELSEA

Saturday, December 28th, at 2.30.

H. PETERKEN, Printer (T.U.), 159 High St., Poplar, E. 14; and at Canning Town, E.16. Tel. 2368 East

Single sheet programmes were issued for wartime matches.

THE SOUTHERN LEAGUE.

	Played	Won	Lost	Drn.	Goals For	Agst.	Pts.
Portsmouth ...	41	23	6	12	73	26	58
Watford ...	41	25	10	6	66	42	56
Crystal Palace...	41	22	8	11	68	42	55
Cardiff City ...	40	17	7	16	67	42	50
Plymouth Argyle ...	40	19	11	10	55	28	48
Southampton ...	41	18	15	8	73	60	44
Queen's Park Rangers...	40	17	14	9	59	48	43
Reading ...	41	15	13	13	49	43	43
Southend United ...	40	13	11	16	42	43	42
Swansea ...	41	15	15	11	52	45	41
Exeter City ...	40	16	15	9	53	49	41
Norwich City ...	40	15	15	10	63	55	40
Millwall ...	41	14	16	11	51	54	39
Swindon ...	41	16	18	7	62	66	39
Brentford ...	40	14	16	10	50	56	38
Brighton and Hove ...	41	14	19	8	58	69	36
Bristol Rovers ...	40	11	18	11	58	76	33
Newport County ...	41	12	22	7	44	70	31
Northampton ...	41	11	21	9	61	101	31
Luton ...	40	10	21	9	50	73	29
Merthyr Town ...	41	9	21	11	47	75	29
Gillingham ...	40	10	24	6	32	70	26

LONDON COMBINATION.

	Played	Won	Drn.	Last	Goals For	Agst.	Pts
Tottenham Hotspur .	34	22	5	7	98	52	49
The Arsenal ...	35	17	10	8	77	41	44
Millwall ...	35	18	6	11	51	45	42
West Ham United ...	36	17	7	11	61	50	41
Clapton Orient ...	34	16	5	13	71	63	37
Fulham ...	35	14	9	13	54	50	35
Crystal Palace ...	36	13	6	17	41	51	31
Chelsea ...	34	12	7	15	56	70	32
Queen's Pk. Rangers	35	7	10	18	38	66	24
Brentford ...	34	4	5	25	35	93	13

NEXT MATCH AT THE DEN—

MONDAY AFTERNOON, MAY 10th,

CHARITY MATCH !

BILLINGSGATE
v.
SMITHFIELD

Millwall v. Crystal Palace.
KICK-OFF 3.30 P.M.

Drawn 1-1

Note THE Bottle.

MILLWALL (Blue).

Right   WOOD 1   *Left*

ALLMAN 2   WOODLEY 3

VOISEY 4   HILL 5   McALPINE 6

H. BUCK 7   A. MOULE 8   HODGE 10   DEMPSEY 11

BROAD 9

Referee—   G. N. WATSON.

E. SMITH 14

WHIBLEY 12   MENLOVE 13   CONNER 15   BATEMAN 16

FEEBURY 17   BATES 18   ISLEY 19

RHODES 20   LITTLE 21

Left.   ALDERSON 22   *Right.*

CRYSTAL PALACE.

Linesmen—E. P. HIGH and G. ROWE.

Spectators are requested not to cross the field either before or after the play

The last ever programme issued for a Millwall Southern League fixture was for the game against Crystal Palace on 1 May 1920. The match finished as a 1-1 draw.

Three

The Roaring Twenties
1920-1928

Millwall Football Club with the Lincoln Hospital Cup, 1921/22. From left to right, back row: R. Jones, J. Fort, J. Lansdale, W. Woodley, F.G. Weedon (director). Middle row: Wilson (donor of the trophy), W. Voisey, J. Riddle, W. Stanton, E. Briggs. Front row: M. Hopper, S.C. Sayer, C. Hannaford, C. Sutherland, J. Musgrove. Millwall finished twelfth in Division Three (South), winning 10, drawing 18 and losing 14, scoring 38 and conceding 42 goals. Billy Keem top scored with 8.

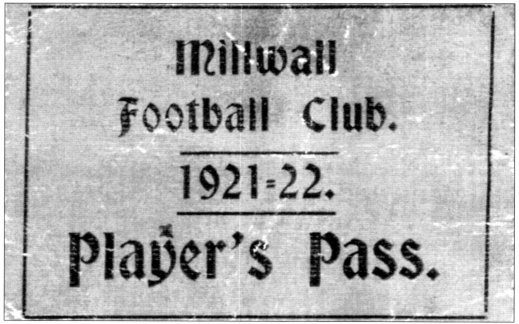

A player's pass from the 1921/22 season – this one was issued to Jimmy Thompson. Centre forward Thompson's Millwall career lasted just 7 games. A much-travelled player, he had started out as an amateur with Charlton and Wimbledon before joining Millwall in December 1921. The following summer he left The Den to join Tranmere, before appearing for a variety of clubs over the next thirteen years, including Coventry, Clapham Orient, Luton, Chelsea, Norwich, Sunderland and Fulham. Other spells with non-League teams followed, before he linked up with Linfield in Belfast. By September 1935 Jim was to be found assisting Lucerne in Switzerland. Thompson continued with football after the Second World War and as a scout he is credited with the discovery of Jimmy 'It's a funny old game' Greaves. Jimmy Thompson died at Epsom racecourse in 1984.

Voisey, Hannaford and Woodley leaping an improvised hurdle.

Now where did that coin go? Skipper Billy Voisey does the honours at the toss-up before an FA Cup first round tie against Ashington in January 1922. Billy 'Banger' Voisey was another local find and he signed for Millwall in 1908. A hard and tenacious tackler, it was, however, his shooting prowess that earned him his nickname. He joined the Royal Field Artillery in the First World War and saw plenty of action in France and Flanders. Billy was promoted to the rank of sergeant and awarded the Military Medal and the Belgian Croix de Guerre for bravery under fire during the conflict, thus becoming Millwall's most highly-decorated player. After the Armistice he carried on his career with the Lions and was in the England team that faced Wales in a victory international at Cardiff in October 1919. In the summer of 1920 he went on an FA tour to South Africa, where he played in three 'Test' matches. After a year at Bournemouth, he went into the coaching and training side of the game and in this capacity he assisted Leytonstone, Fulham, Millwall and the Great Britain team for the 1936 Berlin Olympics. When he returned to Millwall in 1939, he stayed at The Den until his retirement in 1962.

Moule, Keen, and Dorsett attacking the Ashington goal. Millwall won the game 4-2

Millwall take the field against Crystal Palace at The Nest (whose previous inhabitants were the now-defunct Croyden Common FC) in the next round on 28 January 1922. Voisey is leading them out and he is followed by Lansdale and Fort.

Voisey at the toss-up with his opposite number. The game finished as a draw.

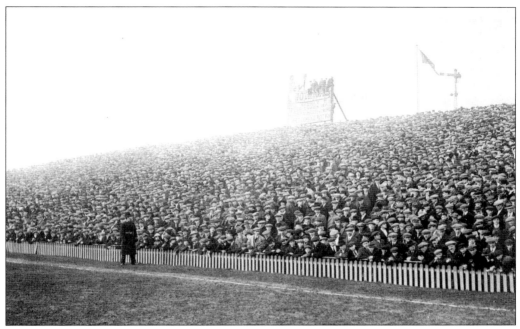

The uncovered North Terrace during the 1922 FA Cup second round replay against Crystal Palace on 1 February 1922. A large crowd of 35,800 watched the game.

Keen goes up for a header during the Palace match, which finished 2-0 to Millwall.

Millwall Football Club, 1922/23. From left to right, back row: S. Regan, J. Fort, H. Tilling, J. Lansdale, S. Crawford, R. Hill, J. Hart, A. Amos, J. Burns. Third row: R. Jones, J. Joyce, W. Voisey (captain), A. Pembleton, G. Pither, A. Layton, W. Moor, E. Moor (groundsman). Second row: G.A. Saunders (director), R. Hunter, F.G. Weedon (director), A. Green, C. King, J. Riddell, A. Gomm, W. Stanton, A. Gillies, J. Beveridge (secretary), J. Higson, (director), T. Thorne (director). Second row: G. Taylor, M. Hopper, C. Hannaford, J. Dorsett. Front row: J. Thompson, J. Lane, W. Keen. Millwall finished the season in sixth position in Division Three (South), having won 14, drawn 18 and lost 10 of their matches, scoring 45 and conceding 40 goals. The top scorer for the seaon was Alf Moule with 9.

An informal shot of a Millwall line-up during the 1923/24 season. From left to right: A. Kingsley, W. Keen, A. Pembleton, A. Gomm, S. Crawford, A. Amos, R. Hill, S. Gore, A. Moule, J. Fort and J. Lane.

**OUR FOOT-
BALL BOYS
No. 7.**

SYD CRAWFORD
(Millwall). The
Lions' new goalie is
a coming Sam Har-
dy. Has had a deal
of experience be-
tween the sticks,
having served in
that capacity for the
Arsenal and Read-
ing. His skill may
mean promotion for
Millwall.

Syd Crawford
(Millwall.)

Harold Sydney Crawford was born in County Durham in 1887 and started his career as a goalkeeper with Hebburn Argyle and was brought south by Woolwich Arsenal in 1911. After two seasons with the Gunners he moved to Southern League Reading in the summer of 1913. While at Elm Park he built up a reputation as a penalty-saving expert and was awarded a benefit after nine years with the Biscuitmen. Joining the Lions in June 1922, he proved a formidable last line of defence. Syd left The Den after 77 League appearances in September 1926 to join Workington.

81

Millwall Football Club, 1923/24. From left to right, back row: A. Gillies, J. Fort, H. Tilling, J. Lansdale, R. Hill, H. Crawford, S. Regan, A. Radford. Fourth row: J. Joyce, R. Jones, W. Moor, E. Moor. Third row: R. Hunter, G.A. Saunders (director), A. Pembleton, A. Gomm, J. Harrold, A. Amos, A. Collins, H. Hankey, F. Crook, T. Thorne (director), J. Beveridge (secretary). Second row: G. Pither, A. Moule, J. Dillimore, W. Ritchie, J. Rowell, S. Gore. Front row: A. Oakes, D. Morris, J. Lane, W. Keen. Millwall finished the campaign in third place in Division Three (South) with 22 wins, 10 draws and 10 defeats, scoring 64 and conceding 38 goals. The top scorer for the season was Dave Morris with 17.

A striker, Billy 'Mother' Keen joined Millwall as an amateur in January 1920 from Chesham, signing as a professional four months later. Bill was a marvellous opportunist, for which he suffered a lot of injuries – which affected his confidence. He will go down in Millwall folklore as the only player to score four goals in an FA Cup tie since The Lions became a Football League club in 1920, achieving this against Swansea Town in a third round tie at The Den on 18 February 1922. Keen moved on to Luton Town in 1924 before dropping out of League Football.

An Agreement made the Seventh

day of *May* 19 2 3 between *Angus Gillies* of *New Cross*

in the County of *London*

the Secretary of and acting pursuant to Resolution and Authority for and on behalf of the *Millwall* FOOTBALL CLUB,

of *New Cross* (hereinafter referred to as the Club)

of the one part and *Alfred H Amos.*

of *West Ealing*

in the County of *Middlesex* Professional Football Player

(hereinafter referred to as the Player) of the other part **Whereby** it is agreed as follows :—

1. The Player hereby agrees to play in an efficient manner and to the best of his ability for the Club.

2. The Player shall attend the Club's ground or any other place decided upon by the Club for the purposes of or in connection with his training as a Player pursuant to the instructions of the Secretary, Manager or Trainer of the Club or of such other person or persons as the Club may appoint.

3. The Player shall do everything necessary to get and keep himself in the best possible condition so as to render the most efficient service to the Club and will carry out all the training and other instructions of the Club through its representative officials.

4. The Player shall observe and be subject to all the Rules, Regulations and Bye-laws of The Football Association, and any other Association, League or Combination of which the Club shall be a member. And this Agreement shall be subject to any action which shall be taken by The Football Association under their Rules for the suspension or termination of the Football Season and if any such suspension or termination shall be decided upon the payment of wages shall likewise be suspended or terminated as the case may be.

5. The Player shall not engage in any business or live in any place which the Directors (or Committee) of the Club may deem unsuitable.

6. If the Player shall prove palpably inefficient or shall be guilty of serious misconduct or breach of the disciplinary Rules of the Club, the Club may on giving 14 days' notice to the said Player or the Club may on giving 28 days' notice to the said Player on any reasonable grounds terminate this Agreement and dispense with the services of the Player (without prejudice to the Club's right for transfer fees) in pursuance of the Rules of all such Associations, Leagues and Combinations of which the Club may be a member. Such notice or notices shall be in writing and shall specify the reason for the same being given and shall also set forth the rights of appeal to which the Player is entitled under the Rules of The Football Association.

The Rights of Appeal are as follows :—

Any League or other Combination of Clubs may, subject to these Rules, make such regulations between their Clubs and Players as they may deem necessary. Where Leagues and Combinations are sanctioned direct by this Association an Appeals Committee shall be appointed by this Association. Where Leagues and Combinations are sanctioned by County Associations an Appeals Committee shall be appointed by the sanctioning County Associations. Where an agreement between a Club and a Player in any League or other Combination provides for the Club terminating by notice to the Player of the Agreement between the Club and Player on any reasonable ground the following practice shall prevail : A Player shall have the right to appeal to the Management Committee of his League or Combination and a further right of appeal to the Appeals Committee of that body. A Club on giving notice to a Player to terminate his Agreement must at the same time give notice to the League or Combination of which the Club is a member. The Player shall have the right of Appeal to the League or Combination, but such appeal must be made within 7 days of the receipt of the Notice from the Club. The Notice terminating the Agreement must inform the Player the reasons or grounds for such Notice. If the Player proposes to appeal, he must do so within 7 days of the receipt of the Notice from the Club. The appeal shall be heard by the Management Committee within 10 days of the receipt of the Notice from the player. If either party is dissatisfied with the decision, there shall be a right of further appeal to the Appeals Committee of the League or Combination, but such appeal must be made within 7 days of the receipt of the intimation of the decision of the Management Committee, and must be heard by the Appeals Committee within 10 days of the receipt of the Notice of Appeal. The League or Combination shall report to this Association when the matter is finally determined, and the Agreement and Registration shall be cancelled by this Association where necessary. Agreements between Clubs and Players shall contain a clause showing the provision made for dealing with such disputes and for the cancelling of the Agreements and Registrations by this Association. Clubs not belonging to any League or Combination before referred to may, upon obtaining the approval of this Association make similar regulations. Such Regulations to provide for a right of appeal by either party to the County Association, or to this Association.

7. This Agreement and the terms and conditions thereof shall be as to its suspension and termination subject to the Rules of The Football Association and to any action which may be taken by the Council of The Football Association or any deputed Committee and in any proceedings by the Player against the Club it shall be a sufficient and complete defence and answer by and on the part of the Club that such suspension or termination hereof is due to the action of The Football Association, or any Sub-Committee thereof to whom the power may be delegated.

This is Millwall's great half-back Alf Amos' contract from 1923. For his services to Millwall Football Club he earned £7 a week during the season and £6 during the summer. A South Londoner, Alf had originally signed for Millwall in May 1922 from Brentford, for whom he had played 75 times. In eight seasons at Cold Blow Lane he would play in over 250 matches for The Lions (including nine of the eleven-match run in 1926 when Millwall did not concede a single goal). When Millwall recorded their biggest away win in the League – 6-1 at Crystal Palace in May 1927 – Alf missed a penalty. Alf won several honours at The Den, including a Division Three (South) title in 1928 and a London Challenge Cup winner's medal after the 6-3 defeat of Leyton on 7 May 1928. He also represented the FA against a Royal Navy/Marines XI. When he left Millwall in 1930, he became player-coach to Hitchin Town.

---

8. In consideration of the observance by the said Player of the terms, provisions and conditions of this Agreement, the said *Angus Gillies*

on behalf of the Club hereby agrees that the said Club shall pay to the said Player the sum of £ *Six* per week from *during close Season*

and £ *Seven* per week from *during playing Season*

9. This Agreement shall cease and determine on *3 May 1924* unless the same shall be previously determined in accordance with the provisions hereinbefore set forth.

Fill in any other provisions required.

As Witness the hands of the said parties the day and year first aforesaid.

Signed by the said *a H Amos* and *a Gillies*

(s) *a H amos*

(s) *a Gillies*

In the presence of

(SIGNATURE) *N R James*

(OCCUPATION) *Trainer*

(ADDRESS) *The Den New Cross)*

Action from the match between Millwall and Swindon at The Den on 27 August 1923. *Above*: Millwall clear a high ball away from the danger area. The Millwall men (in the lighter coloured shirts) are, from left to right: Amos, Gomm, Pither, Gore and Hill. *Left*: Syd Crawford at his majestic best.

The *Football Favourite* cover featuring the great Jack Fort. A short, sturdy, Lancashire-born full-back with excellent positional play and anticipation, Jack was a great favourite with the Millwall crowd. He was signed from Exeter City in 1914 by Bert Lipsham. Jack saw service in the First World War and, following demobilisation, he returned to Millwall. Jack also appeared for the Football Association against both the Army and Oxford University, as well as for the South against England in a trial match and, later, for England against the North. His only actual international cap came when he played for England against Belgium in Brussels. Jack gave up playing at the age of forty-two and stayed with Millwall as a member of staff, eventually becoming assistant groundsman to Bill Moor.

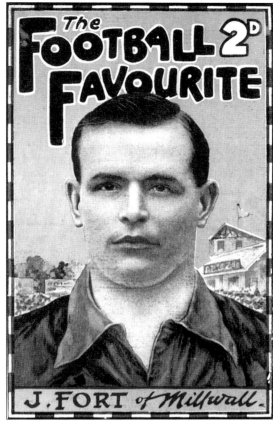

'The Merry Millwall Men' as depicted by Jos Walker.

Millwall Football Club, 1924/25. From left to right, back row: A. Radford, J. Fort, H.S. Crawford, J. Lansdale, R. Hill, C. Brown, H. Tilling. Third row: J. Joyce, R. Jones, A. Pembleton, A. Collins, W. Keen, L. Graham, C. Styles, A. Amos, H. Hankey, A. Gomm, A. Gillies, W. Moor, E. Moor. Second row: G.A. Saunders (director), F.G. Weedon (director), W. Bird, A. Oakes, H. Clark, A. Lincoln, J. Dillimore, F. Crook, J. Beveridge (secretary), J. Higson (director), T. Thorne (director). Front row: W. Battiste, A. Kingsley, D.H. Morris, R. Parker, A. Moule, S.P. Gore, A. Black. Inset: R. Hunter, A. Whalley. Millwall finished the season in fifth position in Division Three (South), having won 18, drawn 13 and lost 11, scoring 58 and conceding 38 goals. The top scorer for the season was Alf Moule with 18.

A cigarette card issued during the 1920s featuring the Millwall Lion

OGDEN'S CIGARETTES

MILLWALL

Bob Hunter came to Millwall in 1897 to fill the void left by the death of trainer Jimmy Lindsay. He came with a high reputation as a runner – for which he had won many trophies back in his native Scotland. With his connections back home there was a steady flow of talent from north of the border, his Caledonian imports including Donald Gow, Dave Storrier and Andrew Easton. However, not all Hunter's recruits would be Scots as he also nurtured home-grown players. This was instigated when he took Millwall St Johns under the club's wing as a reserve eleven, a move that was to produce the likes of Dick Jones, Fred Bevan, Sammy Frost and Jimmy Riley. Bob's continued association with the club went on through the First World War and in 1918 he became manager in his own right. Over the years Bob lost none of the sparkle that enabled him to sign a player when required and among his astute captures were centre forwards Dick Parker and Jack Cock. His connection with Millwall spanned some great times, including two FA Cup semi-finals, the change from Southern League to Football League and, best of all, the Division Three (South) championship in 1928 with what was probably Millwall's finest team. Notice that this photograph of Bob is taken from the right-hand side – he had a false left eye of which he was conscious and always insisted on photographs being taken from his 'best' side. The great Bob Hunter died on 29 March 1933.

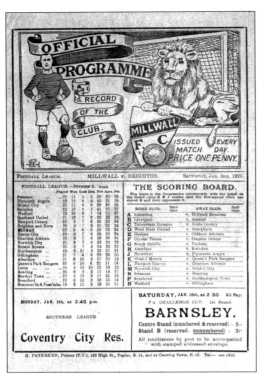

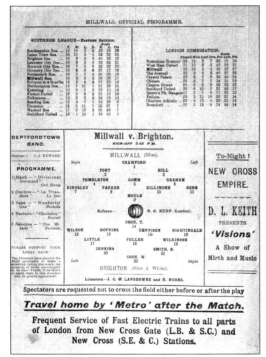

This page shows the front cover (top left), programme notes (top right) and team details (below left) of the programme for Millwall's game against Brighton at The Den in 3 January 1925. Alf Moule scored the Lions' goal in this 1-1 draw in front of 20,000 spectators.

The front (right) and reverse (below) sides of a commemorative medal presented to Lions legend Len Graham as 'A souvenir of the first soccer match played in Sydney between English and Australians teams, May 30th 1925'.

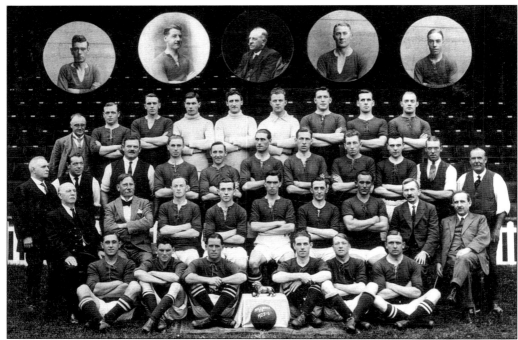

Millwall Football Club, 1925/26. From left to right, back row: A. Gillies, J. Fort, R. Hill, N. Scruby, J. Lansdale, F. Fox, H. Tilling, C. Brown, A. Radford. Third row: R. Hunter, R. Jones, J. Joyce, W. Keen, A. Pembleton, A. Gomm, W.I. Bryant, C. Styles, A. Lincoln, W. Moor, E. Moor. Second row: G.A. Saunders (director), F.G. Weedon (director), G. Chance, W. McNaughton, W. Burley, J. Canner, A. Black, J. Beveridge (secretary), T. Thorne (director). Front row: W. Battiste, J. Landells, A. Moule, R. Parker, J. Dillimore, S. Gore. Inset: A. Collins, A. Amos, J. Higson, L. Graham, C. Harris. Millwall finished the season in third place in Division Three (South), having won 21, drawn 11 and lost 10, scoring 73 and conceding 39 goals. The top scorer for the season was Alf Moule with 15.

Millwall 'keeper Lansdale saves a low shot in an FA Cup tie against Swansea in February 1926. This game gave The Swans revenge for their cup defeat four years previously, as they won the tie with a goal two minutes from the end of the match.

Two newspaper articles on the Lions. One of them explains where the club's nickname came from and the other is from *The Football Favourite* of 6 March 1926.

Len Graham leads the Millwall Male Voice Choir sometime in 1926. Millwall had signed Len as a professional in October 1926 from the amateur club Leytonstone and his transition to professional football must have been very straightforward, for he made his debut, against Brighton & Hove Albion, on 8 December 1923, less than two months after joining and went on to make nine more appearances that season. Len was a ball-playing, classy left half, who could weigh up a situation quickly and turn defence into attack. Twice capped by England – against Scotland at Hampden and Wales at Swansea – in 1925, the following summer he went to Australia on an FA tour and played in five 'Tests'. After trying to make his comeback from a serious injury in 1933, Len decided to call a halt to his playing career. He went on to become an FA coach to add to his cricketing qualifications and also found time to play first-class cricket for Essex. After he finished in coaching he became a publican at various venues around the capital.

Action from the FA Cup game against Southampton at The Den on 5 March 1926. A crowd of 37,928 watched the teams play out a 0-0 draw.

Millwall Football Club, 1926/27. From left to right, back row: R. Jones, J. Fort, H. Tilling, N. Scruby, J. Lansdale, F. Fox, R. Hill, J. Pipe. Fourth row: R. Hunter (manager), J. Joyce, A. Pembleton, F. Martin, A. Collins, W. Bryant, A. Gomm, A. Amos, L. Graham, W. Keen, W. Moor (assistant groundsman), E. Moor (groundsman). Third row: A. Gillies (secretary), G.A. Saunders (director), F.G. Weedon (director), W. Battiste, A. Kingsley, J. Landells, J. Dillimore, A. Black, O. Reinke, J. Beveridge (director), J. Higson (director), T. Thorne (chairman). Second row: J. Page, W. Phillips, A. Moule, A. Lincoln, R. Hinton, W. Burley. Front row: G. Chance, R. Dellow, R. Parker, S. Gore. Millwall finished in third place, having won 23, drawn 10 and lost 9, scoring 89 and conceding 51 goals. The top scorer for the season was Dick Parker with 37.

Millwall Football Club, 1927/28. From left to right, back row: J. Fort, H. Tilling, N. Scruby, J. Lansdale, G.B. Harford, R. Hill, J. Pipe. Fourth row: R. Hunter, A. Gillies (secretary), R. Jones, F. Martin, A. Gomm, A. Collins, R. Potter, A. Amos, W. Moor (assistant groundsman), J. Joyce, E. Moor (groundsman). Third row: J.S. Davies, G.A. Saunders (director), L. Graham, W. Keen, J. Hawkins, A. Noble, J. Page, A. Lincoln, R. Hinton, J. Beveridge (director), J. Higson (director), T. Thorne (chairman). Second row: W. Battiste, W. Phillips, R. Bell, S. Gore, A.R. Caswell. Front row: G. Chance, R. Parker, J. Landells, A. Black. Inset: V. Jones, A. Kingsley, W.I. Bryant, F.G. Weedon, J. Cook, C. Harris, T.H. Lewis. Millwall finished the season as champions of Division Three (South), having won 30, drawn 5 and lost 7, scoring 127 and conceding 50 goals. The top scorer for the campaign was John Landells with 33.

More Millwall poetry, this time from August 1927, to celebrate a home win over Torquay United.

After the Ball.

When Torquay came up for the
   Saturday match,
The door of the Den had been
   left off the latch;
Once safely inside they searched
   round for a ball,
But they failed to apply to the
   owners—Millwall.

With anticipation they started
   to play,
For sometime the ball simply
   must come their way.
Their supporters once saw it
   and gave them a call;
They listened, then stopped, and
   then looked—at *Millwall.*

Now Lions should feel quite at
   home in a Den.
But when in the same place
   they also meet men,
The latter may finish in pieces
   quite small,
Which happened last week when
   Torquay met MILLWALL.

The sad tale is told of the bold
   Torquay men
Who wended their way sadly
   home from the Den,
With hate in their hearts for
   that unruly ball
Which spent all its time running
   round with MILLWALL.

                G.N.S.

34 Years of Striving.

Why Everybody Hopes Millwall Will Win Promotion at Last.

By J. A. H. CATTON.

IF Millwall earn promotion, as seems probable, this season they will be heartily and genuinely congratulated by their old friends in the South and by their new friends of the Second Division, for Millwall have played the game as between club and club—both on the field and in the council chamber.

Millwall's Mascot Lion.

When the Southern League was fighting for recognition as the federation next in power and prestige to the Football League, there were clubs which desired to be members of the older body with its larger sphere, its deeper appeal, and its more intensive competition.

Luton, Bristol City, Fulham, Tottenham, Stoke, West Ham and Cardiff City might go over to "the enemy," and Queen's Park Rangers might have longings, but Millwall, who joined in 1894-5, when nine clubs started this competition, remained steadfast.

IMMOVABLE.

Mr. J. B. Skeggs, formerly Town Clerk of Poplar, so prominently identified with the club in its early stages, was fond of the Southern League, was loyal to that body, saw that his club was faithful, and was apt to make pointed remarks to clubs which did apply to the League for admission, and to those who supported them.

So Millwall remained immovable, were absorbed along with the whole Southern League, and are now hoping to realise by play alone that which they refused to attempt by any other method.

It might well have been a strong temptation to launch out when Millwall left North Greenwich for New Cross, but this club has never been given to adventurous schemes or to "living beyond their means."

NO HURRY.

When the League amalgamation took place after the war Millwall went steadily on. Mr. Tom Thorne, the chairman, was never in a hurry to jump into the Second Division, but the team generally played steadily and well.

Since 1920-21 they have only had one season when they finished in the lower half of the table. From that year down to the end of March in this season Millwall have earned 60.67 of the League points they have played—a very high percentage.

For the last three seasons Millwall have suggested the idea of elevation—even in the last campaign, when they distinguished themselves in the Cup tournament.

In the past seven months they have shown excellent football—save when the ground has been heavy and holding. They have never lost a match at The Den, and have gathered in 19 points on the grounds of their opponents.

This fine performance was crowned when Millwall completed a century of goals against Newport—102 in 33 matches.

QUICKEST CENTURIES.

This feat exactly equalled the performance of Middlesborough in the previous season—the quickest centuries ever made in this game,

although I do not say the best, for Sunderland's 100 goals in 30 matches of the First Division under the old off-side law, in 1892-93, has never been surpassed in merit.

If Millwall score only one goal to-day in the match with Merthyr they will create a new aggregate record in the Southern section, surpassing Plymouth's 107 in 1925-26.

To some clubs it has been painfully clear during the last two seasons that even a century of goals does not ensure promotion, but Millwall have sound defence, and with seven matches to play they already have one more victory than for the whole of last season.

THE BACKBONE.

The strength of the team has been at half-back, for Amos preserves his youth, and any club in the country would welcome the co-operation and the aggressive note of W. I. Bryant at centre-half. Leonard Graham has

MEL
GRAHAM

played against Scotland, and that is hall-mark enough.

These middle-men are constructive players, and that makes the difference between success and failure in any class of football.

THE WAY TO GOAL.

Naturally the forwards must know their business as well.

Now there is John Cock, whom I have seen since he was in khaki, and who then played for Brentford. Cock came up from Devon, though he be Cornish by birth.

He took his place in the Millwall line on November 19, and since he has opened out the game Millwall had scored 65 goals in 19 matches down to March 31. Landells, Phillips, Chance and Black have all been busy and effective.

But the motive power has come from that half-back line, and Cock has been the shaft distributing the power to various parts of the works.

Harford and Hill have been the principal defenders, seeing that Millwall get the full benefit of their activities and aim.

An *Evening Standard* feature regarding Millwall's imminent promotion.

Four
Full Members Club
1928-1939

Millwall Football Club, 1928/29. From left to right, back row: J. Readman, A. Clements, E.T. McCracken, J. Lansdale, W. Cowell, J. Pipe, A. Harley. Third row: J.S. Davies, R. Hunter, R. Jones, A. Gillies (secretary), F. Martin, A. Collins, J. Fort, G. Harford, R. Hill, A. Gomm, A. Hollingworth, W. Moor (assistant groundsman), J. Joyce, E. Moor (groundsman). Second row: A. Dickinson (director), G.A. Saunders (director), F.G. Weedon (director), J. Page, L. Newcombe, W. Keen, A. Amos, W.I. Bryant, L. Graham, V. Jones, J. Hawkins, C. Woodwards, J. Beveridge (director). J. Higson (director), T. Thorne (chairman). Front row: D. Gravell W. Battiste, G. Chance, J. Landells, J. Cock, W. Phillips, A. Black, H. Wadsworth. Millwall finished the season in fourteenth place in Division Two, having won 16, drawn 7 and lost 19, scoring 71 and conceding 86. The top scorer was Jack Cock with 22 goals.

Celebrations after Millwall's first goal against Chelsea in front of over 40,000 jubilant fans in a League match in November 1928. Amateur player W.I. Bryant netted the winning goal in a 2-1 win for the Lions.

Millwall Football Club, 1929/30. From left to right, back row: A. Clements, J. Fort, S. Tyler, S. Sweetman, J. Lansdale, W. Wilson, A. Burnett, J. Pipe, J. Moran, R. Hill. Fourth row: A. Gillies (secretary), V. Jones, J. Forsyth, L. Newcombe, W.I. Bryant, A. Gomm, W. Keen, A. Barrett, A. Amos, L. Graham, W. Moor (assistant groundsman). Third row: R. Hunter, J. Joyce, R. Jones, W. Edwards, C. Woodwards, J. Hawkins, F. Martin, J. Readman, S. Smith, J. Page, E. Moor (groundsman), J.S. Davies. Second row: G.A. Saunders (director), A. Dickinson (director), F.G. Weedon (director), G. Chance, J. Landells, J. Cock, W. Phillips, A. Black, J. Beveridge (director), J. Higson (director), T. Thorne (chairman). Front row: J. Poxton, W. Battiste, W. Corkindale, J. Wadsworth. Millwall again finished fourteenth, having won 12, drawn 15 and lost 15, scoring 57 and conceding 73. The top scorer for the season was Jack Cock with 15.

All Sports Weekly published a cartoon of 'Peanut' Phillips on 13 October 1928. Wilf had commenced his playing career with Stoke in 1919/20 season and, after dropping out of League football, was recognized as an able goalscorer by Bristol Rovers who signed him in 1923. He repaid the Pirates by becoming their leading scorer over the next two seasons and formed such an amazing pairing with outside right George Chance that Millwall signed them both in 1925. 'Peanut', like many of his era, became a darling of the Millwall crowd with his dribbling skills, the effortless ease with which he would go past defenders and his shooting from long range. He sustained a serious injury against the Corinthians in an FA Cup tie in January 1930. Wilf would never play for Millwall again as the club released him, thinking that his playing days were over. However, he regained sufficient fitness to put in another three seasons with Thames FC, West Ham United and Clapton Orient.

PHILLIPS OF MILLWALL - A DANGEROUS HUNGRY LION - DEPICTED HERE IN PLAYFUL MOOD

A 1930 team group.

A policeman watches from the bridge as a massive crowd overflows outside The Den before the FA Cup third round replay against the Corinthians on 15 January 1930, the first match having finished as a 2-2 draw. This game also finished in a draw and the tie went to a second replay at Stamford Bridge on 20 January 1920. This deciding game attracted 58,775 spectators, who saw the famous amateurs hold their professional opponents to 1-1 at the half-time interval. However, after the break Millwall stepped up a gear and settled the tie in some style, scoring four more goals through Forsyth, Corkindale and Cock (2).

Millwall Football Club, 1930/31. From left to right, back row: A. Gillies (secretary), J. Fort, S. Sweetman, A. Burkett, W. Wilson, D. Wall, D. Yule, S. Tyler, D. Jones, J. Moran, J. Pipe. Third row: R. Hunter, J. Joyce, R. Jones, F. Martin, L. Newcombe, A. Swallow, L. Graham, A. Gomm, R. Roundfull, F. Hancock, J. Forsyth, W. Moor (assistant groundsman), E. Moor (groundsman). Second row: A. Dickinson (director), G.A. Saunders (director), F.G. Weedon (director), V. Jones, W. Harris, J. Landells, J. Cock, J. Readman, S. Hutson, L. Smith, J. Beveridge (director), T. Thorne (director). Front row: J. Horton, T. McMurray, W. Corkindale, J. Poxton, H. Wadsworth, A. Black. Millwall finished in fourteenth position for the third consecutive season, having won 16, drawn 7 and lost 19, scoring 71 and conceding 80 goals. Jack Cock top scored with 15.

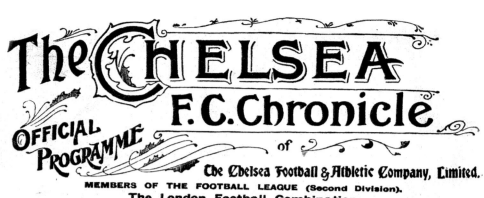

The CHELSEA F.C. Chronicle

OFFICIAL PROGRAMME

of

The Chelsea Football & Athletic Company, Limited.

MEMBERS OF THE FOOTBALL LEAGUE (Second Division).

The London Football Combination.

Runners–up—FOOTBALL ASSOCIATION CUP 1914–1915.

| Vol. XXV. No. 34. | Monday, 20th January, 1930. | TWOPENCE. POST FREE 3D. |

STILL AT IT. By Bernhard Hugh.

Doncaster wants to know if there is a limit to replays.

The cartoonist in the Chelsea programme contrasted the difference in the social standing of both clubs as he depicted the upper class establishment side (Corinthians) playing that of the ordinary urban working-class man (Millwall).

The *London Evening Standard* produced this fixture card for the 1930/31 campaign.

A more informal shot of the 1930/31 squad. From left to right, back row: J. Forsyth, S. Sweetman, W. Wilson, S. Tyler, L. Graham. Front row: H. Wadsworth, J. Landells, J.W. Horton, L. Smith, J. Poxton, F. Hancock.

When he wasn't scoring goals or beating defenders, centre forward Jack Cock seems to have found something else to thrash – this time it's his good wife's carpet bearing the brunt of Jack's aggression. Jack was coming to the end of a very honourable career when Bob Hunter signed him in November 1927 from Plymouth Argyle. A prolific goalscorer, he started out at Huddersfield Town in 1914, but, like so many other talented footballers of his generation, his progress was hampered by the First World War. At the end of the war, in which he was decorated with the Military Medal, he signed for Chelsea in October 1919, leaving Stamford Bridge for Everton in early 1923. His time at Goodison produced 29 goals in 69 Division One games. Plymouth secured his signature in March 1925 and he registered 32 goals in 1925/26 – the best total in Division Three (South) that season in which the Pilgrims finished as runners-up to Reading. This sort of form encouraged Millwall to take the plunge and sign him, which they did for £2,000. This proved to be money well spent as the Lions roared on to the Division Three (South) championship in 1928, helped in no small way by Jack's 25 goals from 27 appearances. He would hold Millwall's goalscoring record (with 77) until it was broken by Derek Possee in 1972. Jack became the Lions' manager in 1944 and held the job until August 1948, in which time Millwall had been relegated from Division Two. When he left The Den, Jack went back to running his public house, the White Hart, in New Cross – not the best of endings for such a great player and gentleman.

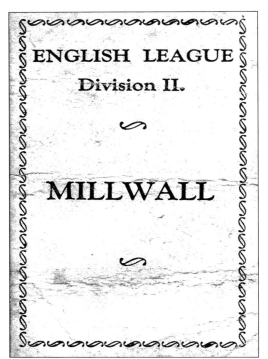

ENGLISH LEAGUE

Division II.

MILLWALL

MILLWALL

Founded in 1885. Played in the Southern League winning the Championship in 1894-5 and again the next season, being undefeated. In 1910 the Club moved to "The Den" at New Cross. They joined the Football League Southern Section Division III in 1920. The Championship came their way in 1928, the same season they won the "Goals For" Record 127-42, losing it the following year to Bradford City 128-42. Colours: Navy blue shirts with white knickers.

ISSUED BY
BARRATT & CO. LTD.
WOOD GREEN, LONDON, ENG.

Millwall were one the clubs featured in Barrett & Co.'s *Football Team Folders* in the 1930s

Millwall fans seeking a better vantage point perch over the gangway which lead from Cold Blow Lane to the big north terrace on 3 January 1931. It was well worth it as they saw The Lions romp to a 6-0 win over neighbours Charlton.

Trial Match Blue v Red. (No 1)

Weather conditions Ideal, cool dry very little Wing

Ground conditions Excellent. close mown new grass giving good foothold.

Attendance & Receipts about 12.000. £397 the whole being devoted to Charity Endowing a Bed at the London being the chief aim.

BLUE TEAM.
Willson, Sweetman, Pipe, Newcombe Hancock Graham Bloxham Roberts Landells Forsyth Poxton.

RED TEAM: Iule Harvey Moran Martin Harrison Brown. Higgins Harkins Smith Swallow McMurray.

Outstanding Players. Roberts, Smith, Bloxham,

Referee & Linesmen. JW Work. RJ Howard, E.F Pickering

Brief Discription of the game.

The Reds started off in a very promising manner and it was soon obvious that the Blues were to be given a good game. During the first half an hour some very good football was served up by the Reds their combination & quick ground passing leading to an early goal whilst several shots test the skill & ability of Wilson in goal. The Blues made progress chiefly by long swinging passes to the Wings Poxton & Bloxham both these players showing good form Bloxham being one of the new men much interest was shown & on this game he clearly pleased the supporters I think the same may be said also of the other new comers

Smith at C.F. showed marked improvement on last years form & displayed some good football in several dashing raids keeping his position & always ready to secure the through pass He should prove useful in the robust game usually associated with Second Division football. Landells for the Blues showed many clever touches but failed to keep his position with the result that many excellent passes from Roberts went astray It is a question that had these two Centre forward change over the Blues would have scored more frequently However it is to be hoped that Landells may profit from experience and blend with Robert & so produce the form he showed in 1927. Roberts showed himself to be a footballer & at least three of the goals came from movements in which he figured prominently. To much caution cannot be observed in judging form at these trial games but one cannot help being impress more or less. I believe this trial gave general satisfaction and hopes are raised and that the teams have every prospect of showing marked improvement on last season.

Alfred Dickinson.

Officials in Attendance SS, JB, GS, JW, LhD, Derbyshire, Capt Jones.

Club director Alfred Dickinson compiled match reports during the 1931/32 season. This example is that of the public trial game of August 1931 and is almost certainly being published here for the first time.

Millwall Football Club, 1931/32. From left to right, back row: G.B. Harvey, S. Sweetman, D. Yule, W. Wilson, J. Pipe, J. Moran. Fourth row: J. Horton, J. Harrison, F.L. Hancock, F. Martin, L. Smith, J. Fort. Third row: J. Joyce, R. Jones, J. Forsyth, L.R. Newcombe, L. Graham, A. Swallow, E. Moor (groundsman), W. Moor (assistant groundsman). Second row: R. Hunter, A.L. Dickinson, H. Wadsworth, H. Roberts, J. Landells, J. Harkins, J. Poxton, A. Gillies, J.S. Davies. Front row: G.A. Saunders (director), F.G. Weedon (director), T. McMurray, A. Higgins, A. Bloxham, J. Brown, J. Beveridge (director), T. Thorne (chairman). Millwall finished ninth in Division Two, winning 17, drawing 9 and losing 16, scoring 61 and conceding 61 goals. The top scorer for the season was Les Smith with 16.

Millwall Football Club regularly sponsored beds in the local hospitals. This picture shows Sir Frederick Wall, the secretary of the Football Association, unveiling a tablet over such a designated bed at The Seaman's Hospital at Greenwich in the early 1930s. The other men in the picture are Revd F.J. Cutts MA and Mr T. Thorne, Millwall's chairman.

Millwall Football Club 1932/33. From left to right, back row: E. Thomas, S. Sweetman, D. Yuill, W. Wilson, J. Pipe, J. Walsh. Fourth row: J. Joyce (assistant trainer), J. Forsyth, J. Webb, G. Ivory, J. Harrison, F. Hookings, A. Swallow, J. Fort. Third row: R. Jones (trainer), L. Newcomb, F. Hancock, L. Graham (captain), W. Moor (assistant groundsman). Second row: R. Hunter (manager), F. Warrilow, A. Bloxham, H. Roberts, J. Landells, J. Harkins, J. Poxton, E. Moor (groundsman), A. Gillies (secretary), Dr J.S. Davies. Front row: F.G. Weedon (director), A.L Dickinson (director), H.C. Moseley, G. Bond, C. Pemberton, J. Horton, J. Beveridge (director), T. Thorne (chairman). Millwall finished seventh, having won 16, drawn 11 and lost 15, scoring 59 and conceding 57 goals. The top scorer was George Bond with 16.

> **Telephone**
> NEW CROSS 1559.
>
> **Established 1885.**
>
> **Nearest Station:**
> New Cross Gate (Sthrn. Rly. Brighton Section)
>
> ## Millwall Football & Athletic Compy., Ltd.
>
> *Members of the Football Association, Football and Southern Leagues and London Combination.*
>
> R. HUNTER, *Manager.*
> A. GILLIES, *Secretary.*
> "The Den," New Cross
>
> London, 20 Apl 1933
>
> *Dear Jimmy. We have missed the patter of your feet on the billiard room floor, in my office & on the field. Haste & get well & gladden the hearts of yours very truly*

Correspondence from the club secretary regarding an injury to popular left-back Jimmy Pipe. A local lad from Blackheath, Jimmy made his Millwall debut as a seventeen year old against Queens Park Rangers on 23 October 1926 and went on to establish himself as the Lions' regular full-back from the 1928/29 season. The Millwall supporters warmed to his play, in particular his perfection of the sliding tackle. An injury sustained in 1934 prevented Jimmy from appearing in the first team again. In all he managed 219 games for the club but never scored a goal. Jimmy was a man of many talents – not only was he a very good footballer but he was a more than useful cricketer and, remarkably, having acquired some land in Sussex and learnt some techniques from books, without any formal construction training he built his own house!

The Illustrated
SPORTING &
DRAMATIC News
SATURDAY, FEBRUARY 11, 1933.
No. 3300—Vol. CXXXVIII.
Registered as transmission in the United Kingdom
PRICE ONE SHILLING.
Postage Rates: Inland, 15d. Canada, 15d.
Elsewhere abroad, 216.

A brave save from Willie Wilson, the Millwall goalkeeper, repels this Fulham attack at The Den in a 1-1 draw in February 1933. Wilson was a Championship winner with Newcastle United in 1927, although his debut for the Magpies was less than joyful when Blackburn hammered seven past him. A fee of £700 brought him to Cold Blow Lane in June 1929, where he had the difficult task of replacing fans' favourite Joe Lansdale. Willie lost nine goals in his first three matches for the Lions and was left out of the next game, not regaining his place until nearly six months later. Wilson probably thought that 'lightning wouldn't strike twice' after his Newcastle debut, but on 16 January 1932, after holding Plymouth at Home Park to a 1-0 interval lead, poor old Willie was hit with another seven-goal salvo as Argyle inflicted Millwall's biggest ever League defeat of 1-8. Wilson was injured in 1934 and never played in the first team again, returning to Scotland. He appeared in 158 games for the Lions (including a run of 114 consecutive League matches).

Millwall Football Club in an unfamiliar guise during the close season in the 1930s. From left to right, back row: H. Roberts, J. Horton. Middle row: R. Jones (trainer), J. Ransom, R. Turnbull, L. Newcombe, L. Hancock, J. Walsh, F. Hookins, J. Pipe, J. Joyce (assistant trainer). Front row: A. Gillies (secretary), A.L. Dickinson (director), H. Moseley, L. Graham, J. Poxton, W. McCracken (manager), F.G. Weedon (director).

Millwall Football Club, 1933/34. From left to right, back row: T. Collard, S. Sweetman, D. Yuill, W. Wilson, J. Walsh, J. Pipe, J. Fort. Fourth row: J. Forsyth, R. Turnbull, J. Murray, F. Hookings, W. McMillan, A. Swallow, A. Gillies (secretary). Third row: J. Joyce (assistant trainer), R. Jones (trainer), L. Newcomb, F. Hancock, L. Graham, W. Moor (assistant groundsman), Dr J.S. Davies (medical advisor). Second row: W. McCracken (manager), P. Higson (director), L. Fishlock, A. Bloxham, H. Roberts, J. Ransom, J. Harkins, J. Poxton, E. Moor (groundsman). Front row: F.G. Weedon (director), A.L. Dickinson (director), H. Moseley, G. Bond, R. Duffy, J. Horton, J. Beveridge (director), T. Thorne (chairman). Millwall finished in twenty-first position and were relegated, having won 11, drawn 11 and lost 20 of their games, scoring 39 and conceding 68. Top scorer was Laurie Fishlock with 7.

Len Graham being assisted off the pitch at The Den by the former Millwall forward Dick Jones and groundsman Bill Moor. Note that there is not a St John volunteer to be seen!

Left and right: New signings Jimmy Yardley and George Phillips get to grips with their unfamiliar surroundings with some jogging and leapfrogging.

Under starter's orders in training during the 1933/34 season are, from left to right: Alexander, Newcomb, Harkins, Turnbull, Roberts, Fishlock, Yardley, Phillips, Graham, Wilson and Pipe.

Millwall Football Club, 1934/35. From left to right, back row: J. Fort, J. Thorogood, W. Hasson, R. Clark, D. Yuill, J. Miller, J. Pipe. Fourth row: R. Jones (trainer), J. McCartney, J. Murray, F. Hancock, A. Beachill, A. Swallow, J. Forsyth, W. Moor (assistant groundsman). Third row: J. Joyce (assistant trainer), S. Chedgzoy, S. Alexander, R. Turnbull, J. Harkins, J. Wallbanks, Dr J.S. Davis (medical advisor), J. Anderson, E. Moor (groundsman). Second row: F.G. Weedon (director), W. McCracken (manager), A.L. Dickinson (director), H. Roberts, J. Walsh, L. Newcomb, J. Yardley, J.Beveridge (director), A. Gillies (secretary), T. Thorne (chairman). Front row: W. Snaith, R. Duffy, G. Phillips, H. Salmon. Millwall finished in twelfth position in Division Three (South), having won 17, drawn 7 and lost 18, scoring 57 and conceding 59 goals. The top scorer for the season was Jimmy Yardley with 15.

George Phillips and 'keeper Willie Wilson practising their art in training during 1934, while also pictured are Jimmy Pipe, Jim Yardley, Herbert Roberts, and Laurie Fishlock.

Laurie Fishlock squaring up to an opposing defender during the 1934/35 season.

This pride of Lions warming up includes the England cricketer Laurie Fishlock (far left), and team-mates (from left to right) Stan Alexander Bob Turnbull, Jim Yardley, Jim McCartney, Jim Forsyth, George Phillips and Bert Roberts.

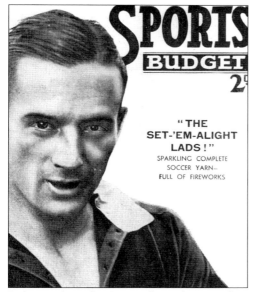

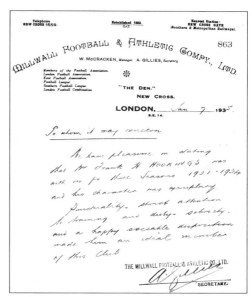

Left: Inside right Stan Alexander was featured on the front cover of the *Sports Budget* for November 1934. Stan played for an England XI against an Anglo-Scot select team at Highbury in May the following year. Born in Northumberland, he played for Hull City until being signed by Bradford City in November 1931. He joined Millwall from Bradford in 1933 and made 95 appearances for the club, scoring 13 goals. *Right:* Club secretary Angus Gillies must have wished he could have had a £1 note for every reference letter he had to write – this one is for the benefit of Frank Hookings to his future employers.

Millwall Football Club 1935/36. From left to right, back row: J. Fort (staff), H. O'Grady, T. Brolly, J. Wallbanks, R. Dudley. Fourth row: J. Payne, J. Murray, L. Newcomb, A. Salmon, R. Palmer, J. Forsyth, E. Jones, W. Moor (assistant groundsman). Third row: J. Harwood (trainer), S. Alexander, E. Smith, D. Yuill, J. Walsh, R. Adams, R. Turnbull, J. Yardley, E. Moor (head groundsman), J. Joyce (assistant trainer). Second row: A.L. Dickinson (secretary), Dr J.S. Davies (medical advisor), J.L. Drysdale (director), W. McCracken (manager), G. Max (director), J. Beveridge (director), T. Thorne (chairman). Front row: J. McCartney, H. McCahill, H. Blair, J. Thorogood. Millwall finished in twelfth place, having won 14, drawn 12 and lost 16, scoring 58 and conceding 71 goals. Top scorer was Jim McCartney with 13.

Jim 'Chisel' Forsyth was Millwall's left half from 1929 until 1939. During that time he made 350 appearances, scoring 49 goals. Jim had previously played for Portsmouth and Gillingham before joining the Lions. He went on to become the trainer at Ipswich, retiring in 1971.

Dave Mangnall, Millwall's captain, getting the treatment of the *Sports Budget*. Wigan-born Dave was recruited from West Ham United in May 1936 for £3,000 by Charlie Hewitt. After trials with Rotherham, Huddersfield and Doncaster, Leeds United offered him a chance in 1927 and two years later Huddersfield had to pay for their folly when they handed over a cheque for £3,000 to sign him. He arrived at Upton Park in March 1935 after a year with Birmingham. Although a veteran when he arrived at The Den, Dave still had a brilliantly deceptive body-swerve that gave him room to shoot with both feet and from any angle. He scored within two minutes of his Millwall debut and was top-scorer at Cold Blow Lane in his first two seasons. However, it was his goals in the FA Cup run of 1937 that hit the national headlines, scoring nine in the competition and in all but one of the rounds. A dispute with the management led to partial retirement from the game, but he re-signed in 1939. Dave hit exactly 100 goals during the Second World War and replaced Ted Vizard as manager of Queens Park Rangers in 1944.

Millwall Football Club 1936/37. From left to right, G. Malloch, F.L. Hancock, J. Forsyth, T. Brolly. Fourth row: J. Anderson (staff), G. Stamp (staff), J. Fort (staff), J.C.R. Smith, J. Wallbanks, J.J. Burke, R.S. Thomas, J. Thorogood, W. Moor (assistant groundsman). Third row: H.S. Moffatt, J. Daniels, K. Birditt, G.L. Birditt, D. Magnall (captain), R.W. Palmer, W. Wilson, E. Moor (groundsman). Second row: J. Joyce (assistant trainer), P. Higson (director), R. Dudley, T.F.W. Inns, D. Yuill, E. Smith, Dr J.S. Davies (medical advisor), F. Jefferis (trainer). Front row: F.G. Weedon (director), A.H. Gould (directot), J.L. Drysdale (director), C. Hewitt (director), G. Max (director), J. Beveridge (director), T. Thorne (secretary). This was to be the season of Millwall's last great run in the FA Cup when, as a lowly Third Division side, they beat some of the best teams in the land to reach the semi-finals. In the League, Millwall finished eighth in Division Three (South), having won 18, drawn 10 and lost 14, scoring 64 and conceding 54. Top scorer was Ken Burditt with 17.

Left: Malloch practising his ball control. *Right*: Hancock building stamina in training.

113

This page shows some light-hearted fun from the ninth Jockeys *v.* Boxers annual football match. This charity match between London's leading jockeys and champion boxers took place on 26 October 1936 at The Den. *Above*: Flanagan, Allen, Nervo, Knox, Naughton and Gold playing cards in the jockey's goalmouth. *Below*: This action photograph from the game gives a great view of the old grandstand, which was destroyed by fire in 1943.

The lads taking a break from training to help erect the big clock.

Chelsea went to the Den to play i
the Cup—and Millwall won 3—0
cup-tie crowd watched. Spectat
appear to be solid for Millwall—t
got the victory smile. In a tuss
ball, players (circle) struck

A newspaper cutting showing the crowd at the epic FA Cup fourth round tie against Chelsea
on 30 January 1937. Millwall's 3-0 victory was watched by 41,503 spectators.

Ken Burditt scoring one of the goals that defeated the Pensioners.

GATE - CRASHERS at the Millwall ground to see Derby County beaten in the Cup-ti

Crowd scenes from the fifth round fixture against Derby. This match set an attendance record at The Den that was never to be beaten as 48,762 fans crammed into the ground to watch the match.

A couple of great action shots from the Derby County encounter. Millwall won an exciting game 2-1, *The Illustrated Sporting and Dramatic News* commenting that 'Millwall attacked from the start and at once it was seen that they were the more aggressive side, while their passing showed greater polish. However, had Crooks, Derby County's brilliant international winger, been fed more freely with passes to his liking, a different story may have been told'. *Above*: Scattergood, the Derby 'keeper makes a vain attempt to save the first of Millwall's goals. *Below*: Scattergood is grounded as a Millwall forward prepares to trap the ball and shoot.

Don Barker was Millwall's inside left during their epic cup run. He began his career as a trialist with Notts County before joining Bradford Park Avenue in 1934. Don came to Millwall in 1936 and made 71 appearances, scoring 22 goals.

Millwall were drawn to face the mighty Manchester City in the sixth round. The corner of Cold Blow Lane, like the rest of the ground, was packed for the big game. A crowd of 42,474 turned up for the match, which was played on 6 March 1937.

Swift, the City 'keeper, tries in vain to save a bullet header from Mangnall as Millwall notch up their first goal of the game.

Mangnall scores again with his head and Millwall are on the way to a famous 2-1 victory. Manchester City were the third First Division scalp that the Lions had claimed on their way to the 1937 FA Cup semi-final. This made them the first team from Division Three to reach this stage of the competition.

J.R. Smith runs from the field in delight at the final whistle, whilst just behind him Tommy Inns seems more concerned with onrushing fans.

The jubilant Millwall fans stream onto the pitch as policemen try and push a way through for the Millwall players.

The players take time out to relax at Blackpool, prior to the big match.

Attempts to get the injured Dave Mangnall fit for the forthcoming semi-final at Huddersfield were in the hands of, from left to right: trainer Frank Jefferies, bonesetter Otaker Steinbegger and manager Charlie Hewitt. This photograph was taken on 9 April 1937, the eve of the semi-final.

The Millwall supporters at Euston station are 'Up for the Cup' on their way to Huddersfield for the semi-final against League Champions Sunderland. During the course of the season the Millwall supporters had adopted a Billy Cotton version of a Bing Crosby song *Shoe Shine Boy* and this was no doubt to be heard on the long journey to the big match. The train fare from London to Huddersfield was 13/- (65p) and a crowd of 62,813 attended the game. Millwall had a reserve team fixture against West Ham at The Den that day and this was attended by over 20,000 fans who were given the latest news from Leeds Road over the tannoy system. One young Millwall fan went to the lengths of cycling all the way to Huddersfield and then back again.

A very poor programme was issued for the semi-final tie against Sunderland at Leeds Road Huddersfield in April 1937. Millwall went ahead after 10 minutes with a goal from Dave Mangnall, but Sunderland equalized on the half-hour and the score was 1-1 at the interval. The Lions defence were heroes that day as they fought tooth and nail to keep the marauding Wearsiders at bay, but with twenty minutes to go Millwall's valiant rearguard was broken and it was Sunderland who went on to the Wembley final (where they beat Preston 3-1). The more outspoken of the Millwall supporters found defeat hard to take and questioned the choice of venue – as it was nearer to Wearside than London – and the choice of referee who was a Mr Davies of Bury.

The Millwall Football and Athletic Co., Ltd.

"The Den,"
New Cross, S.E. 14
20th October, 1937.

Ordinary Shares

No. 19.

To D. B. Thorne, Esq.
"Ivydene" The Avenue, Grove Park, S.E. 12.

Dear Sir (or Madam),

I have pleasure in sending you the annexed Warrant being Dividend on the Company's Ordinary Shares at the rate of 22½%. This Dividend is in respect of the three years ended 5th May, 1937, and is at the rate of 7½% per annum.

Dividend at 22½% on 13 Shares	...	£ 2 : 18 : 6
Less Income Tax at 5/- in the £ ...	...	£ · : 14 : 8
		£ 2 : 3 : 10

I hereby certify that the Income Tax deducted as above will be paid to the proper Officer for the receipt of Taxes.

WILLIAM CHARLES HEWITT.
Secretary-Manager.

This share certificate was issued to the now adult Dennis Thorne in 1937.

Millwall Football Club, 1937/38. From left to right, back row: E. Bringes (staff), T.F.W. Inns, E.J. Chiverton, E. Toser, E. Smith, J.J. Burke, T. Brolly, G. Lea, J. Forsyth, J. Fort (staff/assistant groundsman). Fourth row: J.T. Harvey, F. Hedley, R. Thomas, J. Daniels, J. Sykes, J.C.R. Smith, E. Steele, J. McCartney, W. Moor (groundsman). Third row: J. Joyce (assistant trainer), J. Anderson (staff), J. Wallbanks, G.L. Burditt, K. Burditt, D. Yuill, R.W. Palmer, J.S. McLeod, J. Thorogood, J.W.G. Conquest (assistant secretary), E. Jefferis (trainer). Second row: F.G. Weedon (director), P.R. Higson (director), A.H. Gould (director), J.L. Drysdale (director), G. Max (director), J.S. Davies (medical advisor), C. Hewitt (secretary/manager), J. Beveridge (director). Front row: D. Barker, R. Bower, D. Mangnall, R. Dudley. These defeated semi-finalists built on the marvellous achievement of the previous season by winning promotion and finishing as champions. They won 23, drew 10 and lost 9, scoring 83 and conceding 37 goals. The top scorer for the season was Dave Mangnall with 16.

Millwall players and fans celebrate the club becoming champions of Division Three. Rawlings scored a hat-trick in this 5-1 win over Exeter on 7 May 1938 which clinched the crucial points.

Millwall Football Club, 1938/39. From left to right, back row: D. Yuill, E.J. Chiverton, T.F.W. Inns, D. Barker, E. Toser, G. Lea, T. Brolly, W. Moor (groundsman). Fourth row: J. Forsyth, G. Jones, E.J. Powell, V. Pritchard, F. Hedley, J. Daniels, A. Hoult, R. Dudley, J. McCartney, J. Thorogood. Third row: A. Ure (trainer), J. Anderson (staff), E. Bringes (staff), J. McLeod, B. Pickering, J. Wallbanks, H. Pearson, J.J. Burke, R.W. Palmer, J. Sykes, R. Bower, W. Walsh, J. Collins (assistant trainer). Second row: J. Fort (staff), J.W.G. Conquest (assistant secretary), Dr J.S. Davies (medical advisor), A.H. Gould (director), G. Max (director), C. Hewitt (manager), P.R. Higson (director), J. Beveridge (director), T. Thorne (chairman). Front row: J.S.D. Rawlings, J. Richardson, E. Smith, J.C.R. Smith, C. Kennard (staff). Millwall finished thirteenth in Division Two, winning 14, drawing 14 and losing 14 games, scoring 64 and conceding 53 goals. The top scorer was Syd Rawlings with 13.

Millwall celebrated their promotion to Division Two with a celebratory meal at Chiesman's restaurant. *Right:* The front cover of the menu. The dishes on offer that night consisted of clear soup, vegetable soup, fried fillet of sole with shrimp sauce, grilled lamb cutlet, roast Surrey chicken and sausage, strawberry ice pudding and coffee. Several musical acts performed for the entertainment of the directors, players, local dignitaries and their wives.

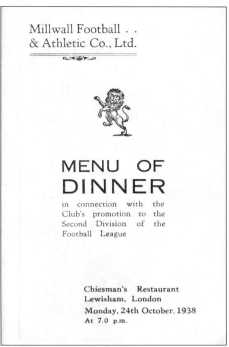

Millwall Football . . & Athletic Co., Ltd.

MENU OF DINNER

in connection with the Club's promotion to the Second Division of the Football League

Chiesman's Restaurant
Lewisham, London
Monday, 24th October, 1938
At 7.0 p.m.

Players and staff tuck into their celebration dinner, no doubt discussing the events of the day, how the new season will work out and, of course, some jokes. Among the players seen here are Dave Mangall, Jimmy Wallbanks and J.R. Smith.

These two photographs show the squad going through their paces in preparation for the 1938/39 season. The new Millwall trainer briefing the squad was Alan Ure.

'On your marks...' – the players are, from left to right: Burditt, Barker, McLeod, Palmer, Thorogood, Bower, Mangnall and Inns.

Millwall's new signing George Williams shaking hands with J.R. Smith on 18 November 1938. Both players were internationals, Smith for England and Williams for Wales. J.R. Smith is currently the oldest surviving Millwall player, living in Hertfordshire. An electrician by trade, he joined Millwall in 1935 from Hitchen Town. A wholehearted player, he was selected for England on two occasions in November 1938 against Norway and Northern Ireland. During the Second World War he was stationed in Scotland and played for Dundee, for whom he would become a player-manager, before moving on to manage Falkirk – whom he led to a Scottish Cup final victory over Kilmarnock. Back at The Den as manager in 1959, he got Millwall playing some exciting football with plenty of goals and a team that was unbeaten for the first nineteen games of the 1959/60 season. He left the club in 1961 to take up a coaching position in South Africa. Welshman George Williams came to Millwall from Aldershot for £2,000 as a full-back replacement for Tommy Inns. He was a solid and steady team man who went on to make 25 League appearances in that season. He played for the Lions on either side of the war, during which time he appeared in two unofficial internationals for Wales against England.

29 October 1938 was a special day for Norwich City and Millwall when they met at Carrow Road, for it was the first occasion that a reigning British Monarch attended a Football League match. Jimmy Richardson is the player shaking the hand of HRH King George VI. A marvellous day was made even greater when after Millwall came away with 2-0 victory.

Action from the game against Blackburn on 1 October 1938. *Left*: Millwall 'keeper Pearson claims the ball. *Right*: Inns is carried from the pitch with an injury that effectively ended his promising Millwall career. Unfortunately, many more players up and down the country would soon have to hang up their boots in the dark years that were to come at the start of the next season.

THE FOOTBALL LEAGUE DIVISION 2 CHAMPIONSHIP.
Season 1939-1940
MILLWALL v. PLYMOUTH ARGYLE
Monday, 28th August, 1939. Kick-off 6.30 p.m.

MILLWALL
Colours—Royal Blue Shirts, Knickers White.

Right YUILL *Left*
Goalkeeper
SMITH, E. WILLIAMS
2 3
Right Full Back Left Full Back
McMILLEN CHIVERTON BROLLY
4 5 6
Right Half Back Centre Half Back Left Half Back
FISHER RICHARDSON BEATTIE SMITH, J. R. (Capt.) OSMAN
7 8 9 10 11
Outside Right Inside Right Centre Forward Inside Left Outside Left

REFEREE— LINESMEN—
Mr. G. V. SEARLE Mr. R. E. TARRATT (Sussex), Red Flag
(Salisbury) Mr. F. H. THOMAS (Eastbourne) Blue Flag

SARGEANT MACDONALD GLOVER JONES LEWIS
11 10 9 8 7
Outside Left Inside Left Centre Forward Inside Right Outside Right
ARCHER HART GORMAN
6 5 4
Left Half Back Centre Half Back Right Half Back
RAE KIRKWOOD
3 2
Left Full Back MIDDLETON Right Full Back
Goalkeeper
Left *Right*

PLYMOUTH ARGYLE
Colours—Green Shirts Black Collars and Cuffs, Knickers White.

This is the programme from the last home game to be played before the outbreak of the Second World War. The match, on 28 August 1939, ended as a 2-0 victory to Plymouth. Millwall's last match of the abortive 1939/40 season took place at Bradford on 2 September, the day before the declaration of war. Millwall Football Club were most certainly a team on the way up by the end of the 1930s. However, the horrors of the Second World War were to put an abrupt halt to the progress of the team that had competed with the best in the country to reach the semi-final of the 1937 FA Cup and won a well-deserved promotion the following season. The Millwall story will be continued in the next volume from Tempus Publishing, which will be available from Christmas 2000.

SCISSORS AND MY SUITCASE

A MEMOIR

SCISSORS AND MY SUITCASE

A MEMOIR

Jayne McCarthy

There is freedom waiting for you,
On the breezes of the sky,
And you ask, 'What if I fall?'
Oh but my darling,
What if you fly?

Erin Hanson

Dearest Pie,

I dedicate this book to you, my wonderful daughter. I hope it inspires you and helps you believe that if you can dream and manifest something, you really can achieve it.

I have dreamt many things, been incredibly passionate about those dreams, and worked hard to make them all reality.

My lovely mom, who you know I miss terribly, gave me wings and let me fly. I'm now wishing those wings for you, as a gift from me.

I'm forever proud of you. Fly my gorgeous girl, fly high… fly!

Your ever-loving Mumma –Muffin x

'Travelling – it leaves you speechless, then turns you into a storyteller.'

Ibn Buttuta
The Travels of Ibn Buttuta

CONTENTS

FOREWORD

I spend most of my days listening to all the ladies who visit my salon. It's part of my job, as I cut people's hair, to hear their stories, hopes, dreams and dramas. There's a lot of counselling involved in being a hairdresser – and I'm flattered by all of that – but the connection runs deeper than just listening. Over the years I've learned an awful lot about the inherent powers of physical contact, the way in which the lightest touch; my fingertips through someone's hair or my hand on their shoulder, can be a connection with their soul; their aura. My job is about caring and serving; touching people's lives as theirs touch mine.

Now, writing stories all about me... that's definitely taking me right out of my comfort zone!

Scissors and My Suitcase covers my career as a hairdresser, which equates to the best part of 40 years of my life. I've been talking to clients for many years about all the various adventures and mishaps that have befallen me in the world of hairdressing: 'So, tell me the latest...' they say, settling down in the chair at my little salon in

Wiltshire. When I've finished, they say, 'Jayne, you need to write this all down!'

Writing a memoir is something I often thought about – dreamed about even – but didn't think I would ever actually do. I'd written out bits and pieces, kept diaries and journals from time to time, but with no end goal in mind and no accountability. That was until the spring of 2020, when my daughter Izzy came home from Brighton University just as we were going into the first lockdown of the pandemic. There we were, the two of us in my cosy cottage, sitting by the fire with a glass of prosecco every evening, with Izzy saying, 'Mummy, tell me another story!'

When she made me promise to write it all down for her, I found myself with no choice other than to start writing, as my secret gift to Izzy.

Taking that leap of faith, not to mention the time and effort, to put everything down on paper is something I'm very excited to have done. I hope that anyone reading this book will find some inspiration in my stories. One of the most important messages I want to convey is that if you can dream, you can live that dream. *What the hell!* I like to say. *Be brave; feel the fear and do it anyway!* I'm sure a lot of people have looked at me and thought, *You're going to do what?!* But more than anything else in the world, I believe we need to grasp every opportunity that comes our way and truly live life to the full. At least that's what I've done... and I hope it makes a good story!

INTRODUCTION

I never wanted to be a hairdresser; I was going to be an actress. At the age of sixteen I received a standing ovation for my performance from an audience of five hundred fellow school pupils and their parents.

It was a dark and miserable November Friday evening and, playing the part of Anne Frank, I sat alone at an old wooden desk bathed in a solitary spotlight as I wrote the last sentence in her well-loved and worn-out notebook.

The clock ticked quietly towards 9.30 pm as I spoke Anne's final words before the Nazis discovered the tiny attic where she and her family had been hiding for three, terrifying, years: 'In spite of everything, I still believe people are really good at heart,' I said.

As the play ended, the lights went out and the audience sat in silent darkness for several tearful, heart-breaking moments. Then suddenly it was lights on and we were all 'back in the room'.

Clapping and cheering exploded across the hall as I stood to take my bow, feeling incredibly proud and grateful.

It was soon back to reality, with an appointment to see the school Careers Advisor. *It all feels a bit too grown up really,* I thought to myself, *I haven't even sat the dreaded and scary 'O' Level exams yet. Anyway, I shan't be wasting the wrinkly old gentleman's valuable time because I'm going to be an actress!*

I confidently and dramatically made this announcement to the Careers Advisor, whose bushy grey eyebrows rose like he'd just been injected with a sudden shot of Botox. He then gave me a deep, crumpled frown. 'There is 92% unemployment in the acting profession, dear girl. Let's find something a bit more sensible, shall we?' he said.

Sensible! I thought, *I don't like that word; I've never recognised that word and, quite honestly, I hope I never do!*

Throughout my teenage years, the word 'sensible' was always, very frustratingly, linked with the words 'school shoes'. Mom and I had many annual battles in the local shoe shop just before the new term arrived in September. So much so, that for the purchase of my final year's shoes, aged sixteen, she handed me a hard saved-up £15 and sent me off on the bus alone to hunt down 'sensible' school shoes.

As I scowled through the glass window at hundreds of incredibly boring but fantastically 'sensible' pairs, my eyes lit up when I spotted *the* most stunning, shiny *gold* court shoes. *Yes, I know the school uniform demands navy,* I thought to myself, *but surely the gold will add far more interest. Wow, it's meant to be!*

The shoes fitted perfectly, were very comfortable (a good grown-up comment) *and* were exactly £15. By the time I arrived home, I had totally convinced myself that the shoe shop expedition had been an overwhelming success and that Mom would highly approve of my choice!

PART I

~ 1 ~

OUT INTO THE BIG WORLD

I left school when I was 17. It was 1983 and I was living in Shropshire with my mom and stepfather, struggling with my 'A' Levels, when I suddenly thought, *I really don't want to do this anymore.* Not that I had the first clue what I *did* want to do, I just knew that I'd had enough of school and that it was time to leave.

A career in hairdressing wasn't something that had ever occurred to me, although I had been really enjoying working as an occasional hair model at our local salon, Michael's Hair Artists. One of the stylists would do my hair and then I'd pose for photographic shoots and competitions, which was great fun. We even came third in the 1984 National Wella Vogue competition, when a really super guy called Eamonn used me as his model.

The prize was a trip to London for a photoshoot, with me all dressed up like an elegant mannequin and Eamonn recreating the hair design he'd used for the competition. There were six models in total, and Barbara Daly, who was very well-known in beauty circles at the time, did an incredible job on my makeup, drawing out the eyeliner around my eyes like a cat, which I loved.

It was around this time that the owner of Michael's Hair Artists, a wonderful Irish man called Michael Thatcher, approached me saying, 'Jayne, I've been thinking… why don't you come and join the team? I can offer you a three-year apprenticeship.'

Why on earth would I want to do that? was my initial thought. *Why would I want to stand behind a chair and fiddle with people's hair day after day, after day? I don't want to do that!* But then, once I'd had time to think about it properly, I started to change my mind. *It could actually be quite an adventure,* I decided. *I'll be able to leave home and get a place of my own.* The more I thought about it, the more I liked the sound of the idea.

So that's exactly what I did; I took up Michael's offer of an apprenticeship and moved out of my parents' house and into my own little flat about 20 miles away. It felt really good to be independent, with my own home and car.

When it came to the apprenticeship though, I wasn't too sure to begin with. My first six months were spent sweeping the floor, serving hairy cups of coffee and being bossed around by the other stylists; running their errands and picking things up from the shops for them. However, once I started learning the trade, things became a lot more interesting. I enjoyed the challenge of building my own clientele base, and from then onwards I can honestly say that I never looked back.

I did, however, find it quite nerve-wracking when I initially started snipping and I literally shook the first time I had to cut someone's hair. I was so nervous during those early haircuts!

Wednesday evenings were 'model nights' at the salon, where we had to bring along a friend willing to have their hair cut by a trainee. I often used to drag my poor old mom along with me, who always battled with her hair, which was really fine, limp and straight. Mom would always insist on having a perm, which I hated doing.

The first time I used her as a model for a perm, it took me two hours to put all the rods in, when it should have only taken about 15 minutes. The whole process was so frustrating that I ended up throwing the hairdryer across the salon as all the hair slipped out of the perm rods yet again. I was so impatient, while Mom was calm and supportive, as ever.

When I first started cutting hair, I always began at the back so the client in the chair couldn't see how nervous I was. Fortunately, I would calm down after 10 minutes or so and be able to actually lift up sections of the hair on top and start snipping.

Hairdressers who are still finding their feet tend to be rather scissor-happy, and once, at the end of one of our model nights, my lovely boss Michael gave me a really useful piece of advice: 'Jayne,' he said, 'you have to remember that the most important thing in hairdressing is the hair you leave on the client's head, not how big the pile of hair is on the floor.'

When I think back to those early years of training, it really was quite difficult to figure out how much hair to cut off and his words have stayed with me throughout my career.

One particularly awful incident, right at the beginning of my career, really sticks in my mind. A client with very long, thick, dark brown hair came to me for a haircut when I was still getting to grips with the thinning technique for long hair, which involves using a special pair of serrated scissors which only remove about 30 per cent of the hair when you cut from the root towards the tip. I stood behind the chair and carefully separated a large section of her hair which I held up and – oh dear, this makes me go hot and cold even now, 40 years later – snipped close to her head using what I thought were the thinning scissors, but which were, sadly, the regular scissors. The whole length of hair sliced off and fell to the floor. I was so mortified that I started to shake.

Thank goodness the client laughed about it. Luckily her hair was thick enough for me to disguise what I'd done. That memory has never left me and, to this day, when I go to thin a client's hair, I always check that I'm holding the right scissors before I begin.

That wasn't my only 'rooky' hairdressing disaster! Having grasped the basic haircutting techniques, I was very excited to learn about hair colour, which was quite a technical matter – back then, I never dreamed I'd go on to become a master colour technician, heading up a team for Revlon Professional and travelling the world!

Initially, however, there was so much to learn, test out and practice: the international colour code; depth and tone; the colour wheel; opposite colours (for example violet will cancel out yellow, green will neutralise red, if a client's hair is too copper, we need to mix up a blue colour, and so on). Then there is peroxide (strength, degrees of lift, processing times); coverage on grey hair; colour correction; porosity of hair – oh my goodness! From natural shade to target shade; how to achieve this?

This is when I learned that sometimes clients may tell you the odd small fib and you have to be a bit of a detective. Firstly, I have to ensure that the colour the client requests is the same colour I imagine and can create. Will it suit them? Will it work with their skin tone? Communication is key.

I learned the hard way when I attempted my first set of highlights. Back in the day, we used a nasty, very tight and uncomfortable rubber head cap accompanied by a sharp 'crochet hook' to pull the hair through. Poor old clients! We would stretch and slide the rubber cap over their heads, which was painful to say the least, particularly if it was a new kit. It would be put on rather like a condom, without the lubricant! 'Ouch!' the client would howl.

Next the hairdresser would take the crochet hook and begin gouging out small strands of hair through all the tiny holes pierced in the rubber cap. Once completed it looked like a doll's head of hair. The bleach/hair colour would then be painted all over the top of the rubber cap and the client then placed under a hot overhead-hood dryer for a faster processing time. Brutal really. Today we certainly wouldn't use heat – and the fumes that came with the heat! Going to the hairdresser's back then was neither gentle nor relaxing.

Back to my first experience, which was all going extremely well. I asked my lady if she had any existing cosmetic colour in her hair, to which she replied, 'No.' I mixed up the bleach with the relevant peroxide, put her under the dryer, set the timer and moved on to do a quick dry haircut in between times. (Dry haircuts... why did we used to do that? Nine times out of 10, the client would leave the salon looking far more unruly than when they'd arrived, and it was really quite unpleasant if you were snipping a greasy teenager's mane.)

I returned to my highlights client, whose face was now bright red from roasting under the dryer. On investigating how my highlights were coming along, I started to panic – with a capital 'P'. My target shade was platinum blonde, but weirdly enough, strands of hair were sky blue! This was awful. I hastily asked her to accompany me to the backwash, praying that when I rinsed the bleach off her hair, she would have stunning blonde highlights. But no, the blue stubbornly remained. On further investigation, she eventually confessed to having put a natural brown henna on her hair a few months previously. That's when

I learned that, because henna is an organic colour compound, there is no guarantee how a chemical cosmetic colour will react when added. My client apologised for not remembering her home hairdressing moment, and before removing that dreaded rubber cap, I had to take my scissors and snip off every blue strand and discard it into the bin.

Fast forward now to many years later, and I was still having the odd mishap! This is perhaps my funniest hair story (although certainly *not* at the time!). It was four-thirty on a dark and dreary rainy September morning. My husband at the time, Nigel, was furiously packing his suitcase and preparing to leave for Heathrow airport as he was flying out to Nairobi in Kenya for an important business meeting.

He woke me up with a coffee and asked if I could give him a 'quick snip' before he departed. I reluctantly staggered out of bed, bleary-eyed, and trudged out into the garden in my dressing-gown and wellies and into my salon.

'Hurry up!' called Nigel, 'I'm leaving in literally 15 minutes!'

'I haven't really come-to yet,' I muttered under my breath as I gowned him up.

Brandishing the hair clippers, I decided it would probably be okay as it would only take me a few minutes and a number two clipper haircut was very straightforward.

I positioned the clippers centrally at the front of Nigel's hairline, and swept across his scalp from front to back. A deafening silenced reverberated off the walls of the salon. Nigel's eyes were suddenly out on stalks from his horrified face, as he stared at his reflection in the mirror. When I looked up and saw what I'd done, it was then *my* eyes that were out on stalks!

'What the fuck!' he shouted. 'You've made me look like Coco the fucking Clown!'

Imagine taking your lawn mower and mowing straight down the middle of a very overgrown lawn. The area addressed would be almost bald, while the rest would be long, spiky and totally out of control. That's exactly what I created on Nigel's head! Suddenly I was laughing hysterically; I'd forgotten to attach the number two guard onto the clippers. There was no way I could patch up this disaster. We had to bite the bullet and I totally shaved his head, there was nothing else I could do.

Two weeks' later we were visiting Nigel's parents in Devon. I was helping his mom serve up the Sunday roast in the kitchen when she quietly took me to one side. Taking a deep breath, she whispered, 'Jayne, I'm very worried about Nigel. Is he poorly? Has he had some kind of medical treatment? Why is he suddenly bald?'

I smiled and admitted that it was my fault and that I'd had a disastrous haircutting moment.

Thank you, Nigel, for being such a good sport. Thank goodness I hadn't made this mistake with a client. If I had, I would probably have been a gibbering wreck in the corner of the salon, never able to pick up my clippers again.

This story really makes me chuckle!

* * *

The odd mishap notwithstanding, I enjoyed working at Michael's Hair Artists and was there for five years in all, including my three-year apprenticeship. It really was a very happy time and I loved my new-found independence; doing my own thing in my own little flat.

By the time I was 22, however, I was ready for a new challenge and happened to see an advertisement in one of the trade magazines for a hairdresser on the cruise liners. The company recruiting was called Coiffure Transocean and, having decided this would be my absolute dream job, I sent off a letter of application, along with my cv.

I never really expected to hear back from them, so when a letter arrived telling me I'd been selected to come for an interview at the L'Oréal Technical Centre in Kensington, London, I was stunned!

On the day of the interview, I caught the train to London thinking, *I'll never get this job; going to work at sea is far too glamorous for me. I'll just put today down to experience, enjoy myself and not panic about it. I'll just learn something from the whole process.*

The first part of the interview involved my explaining what I had been doing and answering various questions about myself and my skills.

Then – and this next part was really nerve-wracking – I had to style two people's hair. The first 'client' was an elderly lady with really short, thick white hair who requested a shampoo and set. At Michael's Hair Artists, we considered ourselves a cut above that sort of thing, which we left to the 'sweaty betty' salon down the road, so my only experience had been hastily practising with a few rollers on a mannequin the night before the interview. That helped a bit, although I wasn't prepared for the model to have the type of hair that she did.

I battled away with the rollers, which was really challenging as her hair was so short and so thick. I finally managed to get them all in, and was just lowering the overhead hood-dryer when they all started popping out at the back. Rollers were flying everywhere, hitting the floor left, right and centre. *Oh God,* I thought, *this is all going terribly wrong!*

My next task was to blow-dry the hair of one of the women on the interview panel. She had really, really long hair which, again, I found very tricky. Still, I persevered and half way through

I told myself, *Just relax. You're never going to get the job because they think you're a really rubbish hairdresser, so don't worry about it.* I decided that all I could do was be smiley, friendly and keep on chatting away, which is what I did.

At the end of the interview, I took the train home resolving to try and forget about the whole thing. I decided to simply put it all down to experience and to try and work harder, practice more and keep learning for the future.

Two weeks later, I had just arrived back at my flat following a long day at the salon – with aching legs and throbbing feet – when I spotted a white envelope stamped 'Coiffure Transocean', waiting for me on the carpet as I opened the front door.

I carefully carried the unopened letter into the lounge and sat down on the sofa, looking at it there on my lap. My big dream of working on the cruise liners might have receded into the distance following the interview, but when I saw that envelope, all my hopes came rushing back. I knew that once I'd opened it and seen the rejection, all the silent hoping and waiting would come to a dreadful end: *Is it a Yes, or is it a No?*

Taking a deep breath, I finally plucked up the courage to tear it open, this is what I read:

22nd April 1988

Dear Jayne,

I am writing with pleasure to offer you a position as hairdresser on board the M/S Sun Princess, to commence on the 2nd July in Vancouver on a 9-month contract.

Please be kind enough to telephone me immediately upon receipt of this letter in order to confirm whether you wish to accept this position.

I look forward to hearing from you.

Yours sincerely,
COIFFURE TRANSOCEAN
(Overseas) Limited
Chris Pike
Personnel Department

I was scheduled to join *Sun Princess* in Vancouver for a nine-month contract starting on 2nd July, sailing initially on the Vancouver to Alaska route, followed by a stint sailing from Los Angeles to Acapulco and back. I was absolutely over the moon, and so excited!

Everything was going so well, until the evening before I was due to fly out to Vancouver from Heathrow. Dad was due to drive me to the airport in the morning, so the night before he organised a small going away party to celebrate my starting my dream job.

At about midnight, I was in the games room when Dad's dog – a very friendly old English bull terrier called Albert – wandered in. I decided to give him a goodbye cuddle and leant down to scoop him into my arms saying, 'Oh Albert!' Then disaster struck. Albert clearly had no idea I was behind him and as I lifted him, he quickly turned and, I thought, just growled at me. However, when I put my hand to my face it came away wet with blood and there was no mistaking the feel of a gash on my skin. *Oh my God!* I thought.

The next thing I knew, it was two o'clock in the morning and I was in the local cottage hospital, having my face stitched up by a very miserable doctor who had clearly been dragged out of bed. What a way to begin my adventure of a lifetime!

A few hours later, my very sad dad drove me to the airport. As we walked into the terminal together to say our goodbyes (me with the new, shiny red suitcases he'd bought me – thank you so much, Dad), he said, 'I'm so sorry, Jayne. Please don't worry, you still look beautiful and I love you so much. Take care now.'

I was so touched that I hesitated for a moment; it was going to be hard leaving Dad behind. 'Go,' he said. 'Off you go and don't look back!'

So off I flew to meet *Sun Princess* in Vancouver. I still couldn't quite believe I was going to sea and it was a really strange feeling, getting on the plane and thinking, *This is really it. I'm really going and I won't be home for nine months.*

SUN PRINCESS
(GOING LOCO DOWN IN ACAPULCO)

I was rather disappointed to be heading off to my glamorous new job with big, black, hairy spider-like stitches on my face, but I soon forgot about it in the excitement. The doctor who'd stitched up my face at the cottage hospital had given me a letter outlining the next stages of treatment for my bite wound and so, pardon the pun, but once I'd boarded the ship my first port of call was to find the ship's doctor and pass it on to him.

All the officers on board were super tanned and very smart in their white uniforms with brass buttons, and the ship's doctor was no exception. Once he'd read my letter he said, 'Jayne, I just want to say that it's lucky we've met today because I used to be a plastic surgeon. If your father's dog had bitten you on the bottom, I'd leave the stitches as they are, but this is your sweet face so it's important. I'm therefore going to take out all these stitches and redo them for you.'

Meeting that doctor was one of my first memories of being on board ship. He was amazing and I was very lucky that our paths crossed when they did!

From July until mid-September, *Sun Princess* sailed in and out of Vancouver every Saturday on the seven-night Alaskan route. On a Saturday morning the passengers would disembark, then we would turn round and depart with a new crowd in the evening.

On the Alaskan route I found myself doing mostly shampoo and sets, which, as I've said, wasn't really my area of expertise, but I practiced a lot and basically just got on with it. There were always a lot of very elderly American women on board, which made my job particularly tricky as they'd all spent the last 40, or even 50, years visiting their regular hairdresser at home then expect me to recreate their usual style to perfection, despite never having met them before. It was quite a challenge really.

These women would wag a finger at me, saying 'Don't you go giving me conditioner now.

It'll make my hair too soft.' I found myself using endless cans of hairspray!

A lot of the clients would say, 'Tease me, tease me,' and at first, I thought, *Whatever does that mean?* It was such a strange thing to say, but I soon realised it was the American way of asking me to backcomb their hair. The first time an American client said, 'Could you just trim my bangs?' I thought, *Bangs? What are bangs?'* Of course, they meant 'fringe'.

Come September, the Alaskan cruise liners tended to move their itineraries as the weather changed. *Sun Princess* was no exception, switching to the seven-night Los Angeles to Acapulco route. So that was me for the winter, 'Going loco down in Acapulco'!

On board ship, the hairdressers were known as the 'hairies' and the beauty therapists were the 'body bashers' – that's just how everybody knew us. As we were all living in a relatively small environment together, I got to know the crew very quickly. I was fortunate in that I was given a cabin to myself, which was great. When I found myself sharing a cabin on later voyages, it was difficult as I would be literally living and working with the same girl 24/7.

I soon fell into a routine on board ship, finishing work at around 7 o'clock in the evening then heading to the crew bar. We usually had a Bacardi and Coke, which was the drink of the moment and only cost about 40 cents, so why wouldn't you?! After a few drinks in the bar, we would have dinner in the crew mess then go back to our cabins and sleep until around 10 o'clock, in readiness for our late-night partying. As we worked for a commissionaire, we were allowed deck privileges which meant we could go out and about around the ship, visiting the bars and clubs, although we weren't allowed to dance.

We always liked to be well-dressed for our evenings out and about on the ship and, being paid in US dollars with nothing much to spend our money on, we would go shopping in Vancouver each time the ship docked and buy ourselves another sparkly dress.

At 10 o'clock, when it was time to get up, we would put on a new dress and some bright red lipstick, then head off to the nightclub. So that we didn't get reported, we had to watch and wait for the last officer to leave before we hit the dance floor, which wasn't until about 2 am. It was important to make friends with the DJ so he wouldn't grass on us.

Everyone had a wonderful time, dancing away until 4 am, then staggering back to our cabins to sleep until 7 o'clock, when we woke up and did the whole thing all over again. How we did it, I just don't know! But then I guess at the age of 22 it was easy: sleep for a couple of hours, get up, uniforms on, back in the salon. Repeat – day after day; night after night.

When I first boarded *Sun Princess* in Vancouver, I made a promise to myself that I wasn't going to have a boyfriend and told myself, *I'm just going to have this time for me.*

That promise lasted right up until day five, when I met the very gorgeous manager who looked after all the bars on the ship. We started talking one evening while he was behind the bar working and I was out and about with the girls, doing our circuit of the decks, or whatever it was we were up to.

The bar manager's name was Richard and we went on a few dates together when the ship was in port. It basically all started from there. Fast forward a few months and there we were, in the back of a yellow taxi in Los Angeles, off to buy an engagement ring!

There were no mobile phones then, which meant no texting or FaceTiming my mom to let her know how I was getting on every day – or telling her that I was engaged, which I announced in an airmail letter!

Since becoming a mother myself, I've often wondered how she felt when I gave her that cheery, 'Bye Mom, see you in nine months!' before effectively vanishing. I recently found some of my letters to her, which are hilarious. They all begin with 'Hi Mom,' before launching into reams and reams of excited chat about everything I was doing, and end abruptly with *Love Jayne* and a hastily scribbled, **PS:** *By the way, how are you?*

The whole idea of getting engaged was very exciting and such a glamorous thing to do at the time. Richard and I were particularly excited at the thought of planning a huge crew party on the back deck to celebrate. It was as if we weren't living in the real world on the ship. We travelled to different places every day and although we were working, we still felt like rich kids living in our own protected bubble with no responsibilities. We'd do our jobs, then go off on another mad excursion somewhere; it really was like being on holiday all the time. In fact, for years and years my dad called me 'Holiday Jayne'.

'But I'm not *on* holiday, Dad, I'm working!' I used to say.

On a Wednesday, the Los Angeles to Acapulco route called in at a small Mexican town called Mazatlán. Here, Richard and I, together with our friends, would always visit a bar/restaurant called Senior Frogs and spoil ourselves with a delicious Mexican lunch and, of course, the odd Margarita. Despite being a very small, out-of-the-way place in the middle of nowhere, in a strange turn of events I was to find myself back in Mazatlán nearly 30 years later.

But that's a story for later on... In the meantime, I was having the time of my life on *Sun Princess*.

~ 3 ~

STAR PRINCESS

When my nine-month contract on *Sun Princess* came to an end, I flew home to the UK for a month or so, saying goodbye to Richard who was off on another ship, this time round the Caribbean. I spent some time visiting friends and family before being offered another contract, this time as the hair and beauty manager on a brand-new ship called the *Star Princess,* which was very exciting.

I flew with my fellow colleagues from Heathrow to the shipyard in Saint-Nazaire, where *Star Princess* was undergoing the finishing touches ahead of her inaugural voyage, although at that point she still hadn't been officially given her name.

The first 10 days on board ship were spent entirely at sea, sailing from France to Fort Lauderdale in Florida, where we were scheduled to dock and pick up our first passengers for a

Caribbean cruise. As crew on a new liner, our job was to make sure everything was 'ship-shape' before taking on passengers and, together with my team of hairdressers and beauty therapists, I had a great time generally sprucing up the brand-new salon and unpacking all the new products. We also managed to find plenty of time to paint each other's nails and do each other's hair!

The bar staff needed practice to ensure everything ran smoothly once the passengers had embarked, as did all the restaurant staff, so naturally we were happy to oblige. We had such a great time, getting dressed up every night then parading down like VIP guests to be wined and dined.

After dinner and a few drinks, it was off to the nightclub where we danced the night away because, of course, the DJ had to make sure his sound equipment was in good working order. The whole thing was great fun – rather mad at times, and also strange in that we literally didn't see land for 10 days.

Things only became tricky during the last 48 hours before the passengers were due to embark.

There were various plumbing problems, and other issues like the Astroturf on the top deck not being laid, at which point things started to get a bit frantic and panicky.

After 10 days at sea, we finally arrived into Fort Lauderdale, which was so exciting. All the crew were out on the top deck, just as the sun was rising. We watched as around 10 or 12 small tugboats came out to greet us, before turning back to escort us into port.

The following day, just ahead of *Star Princess's* inaugural voyage, Audrey Hepburn – who is actually the perfect Star Princess – arrived to christen the ship in front of a shore-side audience of thousands, before she too joined the cruise. Then off we set.

On the third day of our Caribbean cruise, we took a call in the salon from Audrey Hepburn's personal assistant, wanting to book her an appointment to have her hair done. She wanted it put up in her beautiful trademark chignon which was another very exciting, albeit rather shaky, moment for me!

I needn't have worried as Audrey Hepburn was absolutely lovely; just the sweetest, gentlest person and a model client. Timid as a church mouse, she read her magazine, looking up occasionally to see how I was getting on and take a sip of her champagne. There were no airs and graces and no trickiness with her whatsoever.

I spent about three months in total on *Star Princess*. I often went ashore and enjoyed exploring the various Caribbean islands. One particularly memory I have is of sitting on a beautiful, sparkly, talcum-powder-white sandy beach in Barbados, feeling rather down. I looked out to see thinking to myself, *This place is total paradise, so why am I so miserable?* Then I realised it was because I wasn't with Richard. I learned something that day – that life isn't about where you are or what you're doing, it's only who you're with that matters. You can be sitting on top of a rubbish tip with the right person, and be the happiest you've ever been in your life. For me, that was an interesting lesson.

At the end of my contract, I flew back to the UK to be reunited with Richard who had returned to live with his mom in Bristol. We stayed there together for a few weeks before thinking, *Okay...*

what shall we do now? Of course, we had our wedding to plan, but at that time we weren't quite ready for everything that entailed.

'I've always fancied going to Australia,' said Richard. 'Why don't we go to Perth for a year?'

Sure, why the hell not?! I thought.

So that's exactly what we did.

~ 4 ~

G'DAY, OZ

Richard and I embarked on our year's adventure to Perth without having done any research about the place. I guess that's just what you do when you're young! We both presumed it would be a big city like we knew Sydney to be, but we were wrong.

Our plane landed at 9 o'clock on a Saturday morning and by 4 o'clock that afternoon, we'd managed to tour the whole city. It really was much smaller than we'd expected and I thought to myself, *Oh my God... and we're here for a whole year!*

We spent our first week in a hotel and soon decided that, despite being rather on the small side, Perth was a beautiful city.

Those early days were mostly spent sitting on the beach, thinking about the fact that we needed to find ourselves jobs before the money ran out. Then, one morning we were strolling along the

Swan River when we noticed a stunning, brand new resort hotel called the Burswood Resort Hotel and Casino. We went inside to take a closer look around, and within an hour I'd been into the hairdressing salon and found myself a job, while Richard secured himself a job working behind the bar, soon to be promoted to bar manager.

Okay, cool… we thought, *we've found jobs. Ticked that box. Now we need to find somewhere to live.* A couple of days later, we found ourselves a nice apartment, so we were all set.

Perth is, apparently, the most isolated city in the world. Although very beautiful, Richard and I found the area to be quite countrified and very family-orientated which, because of our ages, meant that it was possibly a bit too quiet for us. Nevertheless, we were determined to make the most of our time there, and one of our favourite weekend places to visit was Rottnest Island, home to thousands of funny furry creatures called quokkas. There were no cars on the island, only bicycles, and we travelled across on a small ferry which was all rather fun.

We made quite a few friends in Perth and experienced our first Christmas in the sun that year. It was interesting, and we enjoyed ourselves, although it wasn't quite the same as Christmas at home in front of a cosy fire.

It was while we were in Perth that Richard had a very worrying episode with his health. It happened at a time when we were nicely settled in our apartment, with our new jobs and new friends. In fact, everything was going well until the morning I woke to find Richard wasn't beside me in bed. As I sat up, I heard a banging noise and thought, *Whatever is that?*

I jumped out of bed and went into the lounge where I found Richard lying on the floor on his back with his eyes wide open, shaking violently. The noise I could hear was his leg repeatedly hitting out against the wall.

Gosh, what's happening?! I thought, panicking. I immediately called for an ambulance, which thankfully arrived fairly swiftly. The paramedics came in and gave Richard oxygen. Once he'd stabilised, they took us both off to hospital so that he could be properly checked out.

When we arrived, Richard was whisked off into a treatment room while I was left waiting outside, wondering what on earth had happened. Finally, about an hour later, he emerged looking like his old self again. As he strode off up the corridor, I trotted along behind him. 'What did they say?' I asked, still feeling very unsettled.

He turned back to look at me and shrugged his shoulders. 'They just said, you know, that it was one of those things,' he replied. 'It's nothing. Let's go home now.'

At the time I brushed it off as well. *Sure, okay,* I thought, and believed him. Or at least I tried to. It wasn't until months later that the reality of what happened came back to haunt us.

Eleven months after arriving in Perth, we returned to the UK. We'd really enjoyed our adventure and had had a great time, but now there was the serious business of a wedding to organise!

* * *

As an excited bride-to-be, I'd already bought my wedding dress from a very glamorous shop in Miami when *Star Princess* was in port there a year earlier. It was the first dress I tried on, and quite dramatic, but then I've always been a bit of a drama queen, so it was very fitting! The veil was incredible. It was a big explosion of white net and was very, very sparkly, and very glitzy. I loved it!

The wedding itself, at a beautiful hotel in Shropshire, was amazing, and Richard and I really enjoyed ourselves with all our family and friends. There was, however, one strange episode which I didn't take too much notice of at the time, although with hindsight, maybe I should have?

On the morning of the wedding, I was at the hotel with my mom, bridesmaids and a young pageboy, waiting for my dad so that we could travel to the church together. Dad arrived and we got in the car, at which point he held my hand and was suddenly very serious. 'Jayne,' he said, looking at me earnestly, 'are you sure about this?'

I was caught completely off-guard. 'What do you mean?' I asked.

He hesitated and then said, 'Well... no. It'll be fine. It'll be a great day, whatever.' Understandably, that left me thinking, *Oh my goodness! What?*

45

My dad liked Richard, in fact he was very fond of him, but on our wedding day he clearly felt that something wasn't quite right. Something that maybe he'd already picked up on, but I hadn't, at least not at that point in time.

I soon forgot about dad's comment and we went on to have a really super day, and an amazing honeymoon. We went back to Florida and stayed in a hotel just outside Disneyworld, where we did the whole Disney 'thing' for two weeks. We were like a couple of kids playing together the whole time. We were good at that and a lot of our time was spent playing crazy golf – which sounds a bit weird when I say it now – but we just loved it.

The whole honeymoon was magical and we had an amazing time together, completely oblivious to the black clouds gathering on the horizon.

FEELING LOST AT SEA

When the honeymoon was over, Richard and I both managed to get jobs on *Sky Princess,* once again with Princess Cruises. When we joined the ship in Vancouver to begin the familiar Alaskan route, I had no idea that our voyage together would amount to just three weeks.

As a married couple on board ship, Richard and I shared a large cabin, which I really enjoyed. I soon settled into the usual routine of working in the salon until the early evening, then going down to meet Richard in our cabin before supper. Then one evening, three weeks into our contract, I shut the salon as usual and went down to meet Richard, only to find him in the same state that I had that morning back when we were living in Perth.

Oh my God! I thought, and quickly put in a call to the ship's doctor.

'Stay with him,' I was told, 'then when he comes round and is able to get up and walk, bring him to the surgery immediately.'

Once Richard had recovered enough to get his voice back and stand up, I helped him put his shoes on so I could get him across the ship to see the doctor. As we were walking along the corridor towards the surgery, Richard, who was a couple of steps ahead of me, turned round and said, 'Don't tell them what happened in Australia.'

'Richard,' I said, 'I *am* going to tell them because it's really important and I'm very worried about your health.'

He just shrugged his shoulders in reply, as he'd done before, but I knew he was extremely concerned.

When we sat down in front of the doctor, he asked me to describe what I'd seen, at which point – and with Richard really scowling at me – I also mentioned about his having experienced a similar episode in Perth.

'I'm very sorry, Richard,' the doctor said, 'but you clearly have epilepsy, which means you cannot be at sea.'

I went through so many different emotions that evening. One of my thoughts was, *Crikey, not so long ago I was walking up the aisle towards you, Richard, and the whole time all your family knew about this.*

It probably wasn't *all* his family to be fair, but his mother, to whom I'd always been very close – or at least thought I had been – would certainly have known. I felt so hurt and angry that nobody had mentioned Richard's condition to me. Unless they thought he had told me himself. I simply don't know. What really upset me was the fact that Richard had kept his condition hidden from me and I couldn't imagine why. Did he think I was so shallow that, knowing he had epilepsy, I would run away? That, for me, was the huge sadness – his not telling me.

I knew that Richard had worked on the cruise liners for several years before we met, and can only surmise that he'd become conditioned to hide his epilepsy so he could continue in his job. He must have just hoped it wouldn't happen whilst he was on board ship.

The next day we came into a tiny place called Skagway in Alaska, and this, sadly, was truly awful because Richard was basically frogmarched off the ship by the purser as soon as we arrived, and flown home.

With him gone so suddenly, I thought, *What are we going to do now?* I knew I couldn't break my contract there and then and fly back to the UK with him, as a replacement for my job would need to be found first. I also needed some time to clear my anger.

A month or so later, I managed to leave the ship and returned to the UK to join Richard in Bristol where he was living with his mother. By this time, he had sunk into a bit of a depression, having no idea what to do next or what would happen with his career.

'Come on,' I told him, trying to shake things up a bit. 'We need to crack on.' Which he did, eventually finding himself a job in Bristol. Then it was my turn to look for work. *Okay,* I thought, *where's the best salon in Bristol? Let's start at the top and see what happens.* So off I went, breezing into this fabulous salon in Clifton and getting myself a job right there and then.

I had been working in Bristol for about three months when I was contacted by Coiffure Transocean. They were offering me a position, an exceptional opportunity on a beautiful, very exclusive ship called *Sea Goddess*, where I was to be the only hairdresser on board.

~ 6 ~

SEA GODDESS

At first, when Coiffure Transocean offered me the position on *Sea Goddess,* I wasn't sure whether or not to accept as it meant leaving Richard behind. However, when I told him about the job he said, 'No, you must go.' Then he added, 'Maybe you could get me a job on the ship?' which I think was uppermost in his mind, although I had no idea how he thought that could possibly have worked.

By now I was 26 and, to be honest, feeling rather bruised by what had happened with Richard – his epilepsy diagnosis, and the issues it had caused between us. Needless-to-say, things were a bit tricky at this point so when I decided to go back to sea, I knew that I needed to go on my own this time.

I flew out to meet *Sea Goddess* in Venice and sailed on board her for six months, disembarking in Thailand. It was such an unbelievable gift of a job, and of a trip, because the itinerary was never repeated, we just kept heading east. Guests joined the ship at various different locations, with some staying for the whole six months. Can you imagine – six months?!

There were only 100 guests to our 300 handpicked members of crew, along with our Norwegian captain and his officers. It was super, super, spoily! The guests would pre-order all the drinks they wanted in their fridge before arriving on board, as well as any hairdressing appointments with me, and massages and beauty treatments with Sharon, the beauty therapist. The salon was the perfect set-up, so much so that, years later, I used it as a model to create a similar environment when I designed my own salon in Wiltshire.

One of our ports of call on *Sea Goddess* was Bombay (now Mumbai) in India. Visiting the city was an experience that really stayed with me. We docked in the early morning and, almost immediately, I felt quite uncomfortable arriving at what is probably one of the poorest places in the world on our beautiful sparkly cruise ship, with our moneyed guests sporting their huge diamond rings.

As the only two people working in the salon, Sharon and I quickly became friends and when we arrived in Bombay she said, 'We're going to shut the salon and have the day off so that I can take you on a tour of the city.' Then she added, 'One thing we must do, is gather up any partly-used lipsticks or half bottles of nail varnish, and a few pencils and things, as there will be lots of children waiting for us on the dock.'

And there were… so many children! They all came swarming over to us like a thousand little buzzy bees as we disembarked, begging for anything we had to give them.

Bombay was my first experience of visiting a 'third world' or developing country, and I found it very hard-hitting. It was hot; there were flies everywhere; bins were left to overflow in the streets; and, for some reason, there were men snoozing on tiny narrow window sills everywhere. The most truly shocking sight, however, was the beggar women in the markets with their babies and toddlers.

'What's happened to all the children?' I asked Sharon, because every child seemed to have some kind of disability: there was a pretty young girl with only one eye; a small boy missing a hand… I wondered if some kind of illness had struck the city.

When Sharon turned to me and said, 'The families do this to their own children because they know they'll will make more money from begging that way,' I was stunned; absolutely horrified. Can you imagine being so desperate that you have to do that to your own child?

On our tour we passed a funeral pyre, where we saw the huge scales used to weigh the body against the correct amount of fuel. As we passed, I could smell the smoke from the fire – a huge bonfire of flesh – which I found disturbing. On the other hand, I was struck by the vibrancy of the place. The women all wore such beautiful, multi-coloured silks, and all the smells and textures of the different spices piled high in the markets were incredible.

From Bombay we sailed further down the coast to Goa, which happened to be where Dad's sister, my wonderful Aunty Angela, lived. Aunty Angela, who was a real character and quite the party animal, had visited Goa on a two-week holiday with her best friend, and her best friend's husband, promptly decided it was much nicer than Birmingham and stayed! She would have been in her 40s then and, soon after settling in Goa, met her partner, a Goan man called Val.

Nobody in the family heard much from Angela after that, apart from Dad, whom she called from time to time, saying that there was no need to worry and that she was having the time of her life.

When *Sea Goddess* docked in Goa, I just knew that I had to go and seek out Angela, who was so much fun. With only a vague, rather sketchy address, I shut the salon from midday until 4 o'clock one afternoon and decided I would pay her a visit. I found a helpful, very friendly taxi-driver and, showing him the scrap of paper on which I hoped what was written as was Angela's address, asked, 'Do you know this place? My aunty lives there and I really need to see her. Do you think you could take me?'

'I can,' he replied, 'but how much time do you have?'

I told him I had about two and a half hours. 'No, no, no,' he said. 'We need far more time than that. It's at least a two-hour journey to get there.'

'Okay,' I said, 'can you come and pick me up at 6 o'clock tonight?'

'Yes,' he said, 'I'll be here.' And, true to his word, he was.

By 6 o'clock the following evening it was dark, and Sharon had become a bit fearful about the whole thing. Looking back, it does sound like madness, and I was probably lucky not to have disappeared into the jungle somewhere, not that it occurred to me to worry at the time. In my mind, all I could think about was finding Angela – how could I not, when I was so close?

So off I set in the taxi on what was a very long drive along lots of narrow dusty roads, often in torrential rain. At one point we were crossing a river on a small ferry; me, the taxi driver, and hundreds of locals with their cattle!

When we reached the other side of the river, the taxi driver said, 'I think we're nearly there.'

I looked ahead and, in the distance, saw a beautiful tree festooned with multi-coloured fairy lights. It marked the entrance to the bar/restaurant where Angela and Val were working.

'How long do I have?' I asked as we pulled up.

He told me I had one hour, after which we had to head back. I agreed as I certainly didn't want to miss the ship and find myself stranded in the middle of Goa.

It was very, very quiet as I trotted through the gateway into this magical, really pretty outdoor restaurant area dotted with small tables and chairs. Across the other side of the patio, standing at the bar with her back to me, I could see a lady with long, shiny blonde hair. I just knew it was Angela.

She was still turned away as I walked up and tapped her on the shoulder, 'Excuse me,' I said, 'may I have a gin and tonic, please?'

Angela spun round, 'Oh my God, Jayne! It's my favourite niece!' she cried, giving me a huge hug. It was just wonderful seeing her there, and the surprise and joy on her face. We sat down for a drink and a catch-up which flew by. Then, of course, I had to vanish.

59

Although I only saw Angela for an hour, it was amazing and my dad, especially, was so proud of me for taking the time to go out of my way and find her.

Angela did eventually return to the UK a few years after my visit, where she ran a sandwich bar. I think Val had been desperate to move to the UK, believing, as he did, that the streets were paved with gold and that they would make their fortune. Sadly, Angela's drinking had started to take its toll on her health by this point, and she passed away before her time.

* * *

Sea Goddess continued her voyage to Thailand, stopping next in Bali which Sharon told me was her all-time favourite place in the world. 'It's so spiritual,' she said. 'I love the Hindu religion, the incense sticks and the wonderful atmosphere here. I'm going to take you to what I feel is the most wonderful place in the whole wide world; at least it is for me.'

I've mentioned that Sharon and I became very close during the six-month voyage and we often talked together about our lives. Sharon was married to Sven, the Norwegian captain of the ship, who was a really lovely guy. Theirs seemed like the perfect marriage, spending months travelling to exotic places on such a glamorous ship, interspersed with time at their pretty thatched cottage in the depths of Suffolk.

Sharon told me that while she loved her salon job, helping people relax with massage and reiki sessions, at the end of the day she just wanted to hide away to restore and rejuvenate, not don another sparkly dress and socialise on the arm of the ship's captain. I think she found that aspect of life at sea draining, which is why, for her, there was solace in the soothing, spiritual ambience of Bali.

Sharon's spiritual 'home' was the wonderful Amandari hotel high up in the centre of the island in an area called Ubud, surrounded by rice fields, lush vegetation and the most amazing scenery. As we sat with our cocktails beside this huge, black infinity pool that seemed to drop away into nowhere, I could see why she loved the place so much. It was so serene, and so gorgeously tropical. I knew that some of the guests on *Sea Goddess* were leaving the ship that day to spend a few days there and I thought to myself, *One day, when I've saved up some money, I'm going to come back to Bali and stay here, even if it's just for one night.*

Which is exactly what I did, just eight years ago. However, an awful lot happened in my life in between times.

~ 7 ~

GUTEN MORGEN, WIEN
(GOOD MORNING, VIENNA)

I was two thirds into my contract on *Sea Goddess* when a gorgeous, very elegant Austrain lady called Gerda came into the salon and asked me to blow dry her hair for her. We started chatting and she told me that she lived in Vienna, where she owned and ran a hair salon called Coiffure Bea.

'So, tell me Jayne,' she said, 'how much longer are you on the ship for?'

I told her that I had a six-month contract, with two months left to run. When she asked me what I planned on doing next, I explained that I didn't really have a plan and that I usually just made it up as I went along, making decisions when the time came.

'In that case, let me leave this with you...' she said, before going on to explain that for the last couple of years she'd been looking for an

English-speaking hairdresser to work alongside her in Vienna. 'I'd like to offer you the position if you're interested,' she said. 'Have a think about it and let me know.'

I thanked Gerda for the offer and we swapped details, then off she went. At first, I wasn't particularly interested in moving to Vienna, but the idea kept going round and round in my head until I started to think, *When this contract ends in Thailand, I'm going to leave the ship and fly back to London. Then what?* I really didn't have any plans; Richard had left the UK and was on a cruise ship somewhere…

The more I thought about it, the more I started to see myself living in Vienna. I didn't speak a word of German and the idea of having to learn a new language really appealed to me. I'd always been so impressed by my colleagues on board ship who could click effortlessly in and out of different languages. It seemed so cool and clever, and was something I really wanted to do. *Alright,* I said to myself, *let's do it. Let's give this a go then!*

Gerda was thrilled when I told her that I'd like to accept her offer. 'I'm *so* pleased you're coming,' she said enthusiastically. She then told me that an elderly lady who had been a good friend of hers had recently passed away, leaving her apartment free. 'I'm very close to the family,' she said, 'so you'll be more than welcome to stay there.'

With a job and an apartment, there was nothing holding me back.

I arrived in Vienna and rocked up at the apartment, only to discover that it was slightly outside the city centre and, if I'm honest, in a rather broken down, poor district. As I stepped inside, I was disappointed at how dark, damp and depressing it was: *Oh my God, what have I let myself in for?!* I thought. Had I been tuned into my spiritual side back then, I would have cleansed the air by burning some dried white sage to make the atmosphere softer and kinder. In the event, I just had to get on with it and make the best of things.

I started work at the salon the next day, feeling very nervous. I needn't have worried, however, as everything turned out fine. Gerda was very welcoming and really happy to see me. She sat me down in the staff room for a coffee and a chat, then introduced me to the other seven members of staff, none of whom spoke any English at all.

At first it was all rather strange and a bit difficult. The other girls in the salon were all young, like me, but I found it frustrating that we couldn't communicate with one another. I couldn't even say *guten Morgen* or *auf wiedersehen* – nothing. I felt rather disheartened, then I told myself sternly: *You've made this commitment, so you're going to make it work.*

Before taking up the position, I'd set myself the goal of staying in Vienna for at least a year and learning to speak German. Now I was determined to stay the course and make it happen.

I spent five days a week working in the salon, and three nights learning German. After work, I took the underground and headed to the language school in the city centre, where I spent two and a half hours learning German. It was quite intense, but I really wanted to be able to speak the language as quickly as possible.

My first role in the salon was to build a mostly ex-pat clientele base. We were very close to the Vienna International Centre, or Uno City, which is similar to the United Nations and surrounded by all the various embassies. Gerda came up with the brilliant idea of producing an introductory flyer to send out to all the nearby international organisations, with my photograph and some information on my background and hairdressing skills.

My list for the day soon started filling up with both ex-pats and lovely Viennese clients, most of whom seemed to have a penchant for either bright red or bright orange hair, regardless of their skin tone! Sometimes it felt like I was back in London as I spent a lot of my time nattering away in English.

Initially, all I really needed to be able to do in terms of my German was ask the local Viennese ladies a few hair-related questions and pray, firstly that they would understand me, and, secondly, and more importantly, that I'd be able to understand their replies. My learning was complicated by the fact that the language school taught *Hochdeutsch*, or high German, whilst everyone in Vienna spoke with a regional accent which I found quite hard to decipher. It was like learning the Queen's English here, then finding yourself living in Yorkshire or Liverpool. Still, I got on with it and after about six months found I could chat away quite happily to the other hairdressers. I also managed fairly well with the Viennese ladies, who all thought I was a bit of a novelty.

One of the biggest lessons I learned, however, was the power of non-verbal communication, particularly body language, which is a language in itself. I soon discovered that a squeeze on the shoulder and the phrase, 'I can't really gossip too much, but your hair will be great,' worked wonders and nobody ever complained.

Day-to-day, my work in the salon ran very smoothly and I honestly can't think of any scary moments or hair disasters. The atmosphere was generally friendly and kind, albeit rather smoky – we're talking back in the days where everyone, or so it seemed, enjoyed a cigarette.

Overall, I was very proud of my achievements; settling into a new country and learning a new language. However, after six months of relentlessly learning German, I was beginning to feel rather exhausted. Every evening I would come home to my rather dark and dingy apartment, put the news on while I made my supper and then think to myself, *Oh no! I can't listen to this... I can't hear one more word of German, I'm going to go mad!* and switch the tv off again.

A dramatic turning point in my language-learning came when I actually started dreaming in German, where, of course, I spoke beautifully with pitch-perfect pronunciation. Learning a new language from scratch made me appreciate just how nerve-wracking it can be to open your mouth and start speaking, but it's something you really have to take the plunge and try. So many people think they need to be virtually fluent before giving it a go, but I soon learned that you have to trust your instincts, take a deep breath and let the words come out. It's so rewarding when somebody actually understands what you're saying, and you can understand their reply.

One of my jobs at the salon was to count up all the takings at the end of the day, which I always did in German. In fact, I was so in the habit of counting in German, that I found myself muttering *eins, zwei, drei…* when I counted back home in the UK. There were even some numbers that, when I first returned home, I couldn't remember the word for in English!

At weekends I often received invitations to drinks parties and social events at the various embassies. The mad Australians, in particular, used to invite me over on a Friday night, which is how I came to meet Jenny and Mike, a married Australian couple who were in Vienna on a posting. Jenny was quite high up in the embassy and consequently Mike became the househusband (he also started drinking far too much gluhwein and beer, but that's another story!). They had an amazing rooftop apartment in the centre of Vienna which came with the embassy job. My apartment was one of the few downsides of living in Vienna. I put up with it for a year, then, following a nasty bout of pneumonia, I knew it was time to move.

It was January when I first became ill, with what I assumed was just a bad cold. The cold developed into bronchitis, but I kept pushing myself, thinking I'd be fine if I kept taking the antibiotics. I was desperate not to have any time off work as I dreaded the thought of being alone in my miserable apartment all day.

I finally realised I'd pushed myself a step too far when I woke up one dark, snowy January Saturday morning feeling like I was going to die. Struggling to breathe, it was all I could do to heave myself up onto my pillow. That's when I knew I had to get myself to the hospital – or the *krankenhaus* (I love that word!) – which was a two-mile walk away in the bitter cold. Bundling myself up in four or five layers, I knew I had no other option other than to set off on foot through the snow.

Nobody spoke English at the krankenhaus, and I didn't know the words for 'my chest really hurts, I feel awful and I want to cry'. When at last I was able to make myself understood, a set of x-rays showed that I was, indeed, very sick with pneumonia. The doctor told me that I had two choices: I could stay in the krankenhaus for two weeks; or I could go home, rest, and stay in bed.

Neither option was appealing in the least, but I decided that going back to the apartment was better than spending a fortnight in hospital, and so armed with medication and this special powder for making into a hot drink, I took myself back to my sad little apartment and climbed into bed.

The next couple of weeks passed like I was in a time-warp. Day merged with night and as the hours ticked by, the only interruption came from dear Gerda, who knocked on the door with food to try and tempt me. It was so kind of her, but I just used to think *Oh Mom, I wish you were here!* We need our moms the most when we're sick and I felt like a child again, desperate for someone to come and make me a cup of tea and give me a hug.

I was terribly lonely holed up in the apartment and, as soon as I felt well again, I was desperate to move. At this point, Jenny and Mike came to my rescue. They invited me to share their apartment with them and I jumped at the chance. From then onwards, life in Vienna was really great.

Jenny and Mike's apartment was party town! I made lots of new friends, in particular Alan, a really great British guy on a posting with Citibank, who was great fun to be around. He lived in a beautiful, green marble apartment right in the centre of the city; I assume these lovely apartments all came with the jobs. Being 10 years older than me, Alan was, and still is, like an older brother, always looking out for me. He met his wife, an Austrian lady called Veronica, in Vienna and they had a very glamorous wedding with lots of champagne and dancing.

Living in Vienna was a tough learning curve. I was desperate to make a success of my time there, but soon realised that I was going to have to really toughen up if I was going to make it work. I had some super times, but also some very difficult ones, like the three-night L'Oréal training course in the Tyrol, where I was incredibly homesick.

It all came about one afternoon when the dishy L'Oréal sales rep came into the salon. He used to pop in once a month to show us all the latest groovy shampoos and hair colours, then on one visit he said to Gerda, 'As you're such a good client, would you like to send a member of your staff on a complimentary "train the trainer" weekend?'

Gerda jumped at the chance and who did she pick? Me, of course!

The Tyrol is such a beautiful part of the country and, at the time, my attending the course seemed like the perfect opportunity to meet other stylists whilst immersing myself in the language and culture. I'm sure Gerda thought I would really enjoy myself and, as it never occurred to me to turn down the offer, I said, 'That's really kind of you, thanks. I'll go.'

Oh dear, but it was awful! The sales rep picked me up on the Sunday afternoon and drove us all the way there in his car. In terms of my speaking German, by this point I could just about get by in the working world of hair, but random chitchat and colloquialisms were all a bit beyond me. The sales rep spoke a small amount of English, but trying to make small-talk for two hours was hard and the whole journey felt rather strained.

When we finally arrived at this beautiful hotel, there were 39 Viennese hairdressers – and me. At first, nobody knew that I was a Brit, but of course it was obvious as soon as I started speaking.

There was a lot of role play involved in the course, often with two students up on stage, with one acting as the client and the other as the stylist. Fortunately, I managed to get through that part of the course fairly successfully.

Generally-speaking the days were fine, with everyone being kind and looking out for me; however, I really struggled during the evenings. When I came down to the bar it was always loud and busy, with people standing around chatting in groups, or sitting at tables together. Their chatter was quick, lively and, for me, largely incomprehensible.

I've never, ever felt lonely when I've been by myself, but I can honestly say that those evenings in the Tyrol were the loneliest I've ever spent in my whole life, despite being surrounded by so many people. If I had to pinpoint a moment during my time in Vienna when I felt it would have been easier to have just gone home, it was then. In fact, on the last night of the course I just couldn't face going to the bar and told one of the hairdressers that I was – here's my favourite word again – 'krank'. 'Ich bin krank,' I said, and stayed in my room.

Nevertheless, I managed to get through the whole course and when it was all over, I felt very pleased with myself for making the effort and sticking it out. I even managed to pass and get my diploma, although possibly not with flying colours!

* * *

Towards the end of my time in Vienna, on Valentine's night to be precise, I was in Jenny and Mike's wonderful apartment when I suddenly thought, *Crickey! I haven't seen Richard in nearly two years.* There'd been no communication between us at all, nothing. *Gosh,* I thought, *we've been apart all this time. We should meet up, or at least chat, and probably sign on the dotted line.*

I then did a bit of digging and managed to locate Richard. He was working for one of the Intercontinental hotels on Gloucester Road in

London, doing his usual bar manager stuff. Late one evening I finally decided to try and call him. The hotel reception answered and put me through to his office. It was Richard himself who picked up the phone.

'Oh, hi Richard,' I said. 'It's me; it's Jayne.'

'Hiya, darlin', how ya doin'?' he said, in his usual laid-back way. I told him that I was fine; busy, and currently living in Vienna.

'Listen,' I said, 'it's been nearly two years so maybe it's time for us to meet up and decide what we're doing?'

Richard agreed and said that he'd give it some thought. I put the phone down thinking that, if nothing else, at least I knew where he was and that he was okay. Then the following day – it was a Wednesday – he called me back and said, 'Hi darlin', I'm going to fly out to Vienna to see you. I'll be there on Friday night, staying at the Intercontinental Hotel near Stadtpark. See you around 7 pm in the cocktail lounge?'

'Sure,' I agreed. It was all very sudden, but what else could I do?

I finished work late on the Friday afternoon and jumped straight on the underground. I started to feel rather shaky and I told myself I was being ridiculous. I was going to meet my *husband* for goodness' sake... the only thing was, I hadn't seen him in two years!

I pulled myself together as I walked through the main doors of the Intercontinental and went into the lobby. To the side was a beautiful, American-style cocktail bar with a bartender standing behind the bar. Sitting up at the bar with his back to the door was just one man. I knew straight away that it was Richard.

I trotted up and tapped him on the back: 'Hi,' I said nervously.

He spun round to face me. 'Hi!' he said. 'Sit down, darlin'. What would you like to drink? Shall we start off with some champagne?!' And that was it. Off we went again.

The last two years fell away as Richard and I reconnected just like the best friends and party animals we'd always been when we were together. We went out and about around Vienna that night, enjoying a super spoily supper and cocktails, then dancing until 2 am, and finally winding up at his luxury hotel room at the Intercontinental.

There was a lot of fun, laughter, and generally being mad and crazy together that weekend, as well as some more tearful moments. By the time Monday morning came round, Richard said, 'Right, I have to go now, but how about you come back to London? I really don't want to sign on the dotted line and get divorced.'

I agreed. 'No, I don't either,' I said, and I told him that I would come back to London as soon as I could.

Three weeks later, I handed in my notice at work and left Vienna for London. Gerda, who was really sorry to see me go (as was everyone at the salon), wrote me the nicest, kindest reference:

From the outset, due to Jayne's extremely pleasant personality and her efficient and professional approach to work, she emerged as a much-demanded and well-liked person amongst our clients. Her performance is nothing less than excellent. Her enthusiasm for the work is very high and she always shows ability and willingness to work under great pressure.

To keep abreast with innovations in our industry, Jayne attended eagerly any relevant seminars or supplier demonstrations as and when offered to her, both within working hours and in her own private time.

To her colleagues, she built a high level of respect, motivation and dependency. Periodically, on my absence from the company, either for business or on company leave, Jayne managed the business with all her entrusted responsibilities to my full and highest satisfaction.

Jayne is leaving us of her own accord. We wish her well on her future ventures and strongly recommend her for any applicable senior position available to her, appreciating fully that from the outset Jayne will be able to produce the same good relationships and become a very and most valued asset to any other company.

I was given lots of thoughtful farewell gifts and cards and they threw me a goodbye drinks party;

they were all so kind and I was sad to leave. My two years in Vienna had been a real adventure, but now I was ready to leave and re-start my life with Richard.

Auf wiedersehen, Vienna.

~ 8 ~

LONDON CALLING

Richard was still living at the Intercontinental hotel, so when I arrived back in London we started flat-hunting straight away and managed to find ourselves a great little place in Bayswater. The rent, even back then, was expensive for a small maisonette. We loved it though, and set up home there together.

Having found a place to live, I now had to sort myself out with another job. I decided to start at the top – of course, because that's what I always do! – so I breezed into Harrods and went straight up to their hair salon on the fifth floor.

The place was huge and, of course, all very smart and top-drawer, however, I wasn't to be deterred and trotted straight up to the reception desk where I picked up some of their very fancy brochures to take home and have a flick through. This is what I read:

Harrods has arguably the finest and best-equipped hair and beauty salon in the world, where you can indulge yourself in the ultimate range of therapeutic, regenerative and luxurious beauty treatments, as well as having the most expert hairdressing and colour technicians […] Our aim is to ensure your time with us is a wonderful experience […] Our dedicated team of hair and beauty experts looks forward to serving you.

Although the brochure was a little intimidating, I loved the way Harrods introduced the salon and everything on offer there. *Hey, what the hell…* I told myself. *Feel the fear and do it anyway!* I decided I had nothing to lose, so the next day, back I went, ready to wing it and take a chance. I went back to the fifth floor and asked to speak to the manageress, who duly appeared and invited me to sit down and have a chat with her. At the end of my informal 'interview', she offered me a job – right there and then.

'Start next Monday,' she said. And that was that!

I worked in the salon at Harrods for about a year. It was an exceptionally busy place, with a staff of 30 beauty therapists, 45 hairdressers and 10 colour technicians, although not everybody worked at the same time. There were also 12 receptionists; six permanently on the front desk working with clients coming into the salon, and six working behind the scenes, booking future appointments. The phones were so busy, so 'red hot' that 250 calls were dropped every single day, simply because the sheer incoming volume meant the receptionists couldn't get to every call in time so people gave up waiting and hung up. Despite being probably one of the most expensive places in the country to get your hair done, it was manically busy throughout the whole of every working day.

I actually found it quite hard working in Harrods as a hairdresser. Almost every client came to the chair full of impossible expectations, and sometimes I just felt like saying, 'Um… actually, I'm a hair technician, I'm not a magician. I don't have a magic wand to give you the look you want to make you look completely different.'

Various celebrity hairdressers would put in appearances at the salon from time to time, which made the work of the stylists quite tricky. At one point, Andrew Collinge worked with us. He would sit the client down for the initial consultation, discuss the cut, colour and various treatments available, then, when all the decisions had been made, he'd hand the client over to another stylist – often me – to fulfil all the promises he'd made. The problem was, people have different expectations, and clients, hopeful of Andrew Collinge styling their fine, thin hair into a long, thick, luscious mane would be disappointed when another stylist was brought in to do what was, in effect, an unrealistic and unachievable job. That was always a tough one.

There was, as you can imagine, much waving of platinum credit cards and wailing if one hair dared to be slightly out of place. You'd honestly think their whole world had collapsed!

We did, however, have some lovely clients, Judy Dench being one of them. She came in fairly regularly, although sadly I didn't get the opportunity to cut her hair. However, she was a wonderful, beautiful, fairly quiet lady.

My worst experience at Harrods was with an Irish client. As she came into the salon, and this is awful to say (and I never want to judge people), it struck me straightaway that she really didn't look like the type of client we were used to seeing. Still, she was booked onto my list for a cut and colour that afternoon, so I welcomed her as she arrived and took her through to the salon, where she ordered herself a glass of champagne and a plate of smart sandwiches. We talked through what she wanted done with her hair and she told me she was looking for a new look, with a completely different cut and colour.

Everything seemed to be going well during the two hours I spent working on her hair. She was very charming, appreciative and gracious about everything, until I brought my apprentice over to sort out the payment and get her signature. At this point she turned into a real 'Jekyll and Hyde' character, turning from an adorable middle-aged lady into what I can only describe as a monster. As she stood up from the chair, she started shouting and screaming: 'What do you think you've done to me?! What have you done to my hair?! I hate it! There's no way I'm paying for this!'

As you'd expect from Harrods, it had been an expensive cut and colour, however she'd agreed all the costs during our initial consultation. Now, she was declaring that she wasn't going to be paying for any of it. The whole thing became completely out of hand and she actually threw herself down on the floor in the middle of the salon. In Harrods – can you imagine?! The whole area, which had been really bustling and busy, suddenly went quiet, with everyone turning round to stare at her. Someone called security, who managed to get her up off the floor and into one of the private rooms used for Muslim ladies who mustn't be seen in public without a hijab.

The upshot was that this client was escorted off the premises once she'd calmed down, although not without grabbing a handful of pennies from her purse and throwing them down on the floor in rage as she left. Once her full identity was established, it transpired that she had a history of this type of behaviour. Even so, the whole experience was really traumatic for me; it was simply awful. I just couldn't get over how a person could be so sweet, charming and chatty one moment, and so ghastly the next. A few minutes after she left, a very wealthy Middle-Eastern princess breezed in and headed straight for the La Prairie table, where she spent £5,000 on skincare. What a contrast!

Working at Harrods proved to be a really good learning experience for me, although I knew early on that it wasn't somewhere I wanted to stay long term. The clients were all very precious about their hair, with so many of them asking for a complete re-style, then only allowing me to take a millimetre off the bottom. That was always a really tricky one – and it happened so often! *Oh, I'd really like to look completely different, so if you could just snip the ends off for me,* they'd say, and I'd be thinking, *Oh, kill me now…*

All the time I was at Harrods, I was living with Richard in our flat in Bayswater. Despite never having much money to speak of, we still managed to have a really great time. It was strange, catching the tube to work in the morning with just enough cash on me to buy my ticket, then walking into one of the most expensive and prestigious establishments in the world.

Fortunately, I knew that by the end of the day I'd have at least £20 worth of tips in my purse: that was one of the best things about working in Harrods.

Richard and I lived in the rented flat for a year or so, before buying a place of our own in Tottenham Hale.

After a year at Harrods, I decided it was time to move on. I was flicking through the *Hairdresser's Journal* (the go-to magazine of the trade), as you did years ago, when I saw a UK technician job advertised by Revlon Professional. *Right,* I thought to myself, *I'm going to apply for that.* Which I did. And I got the job!

As a UK technician, part of my job was to train salon staff in the use of Revlon products, which meant my having to go on a special training course to learn about all the different products that the Revlon team sold to salons: colours, perms, hair relaxers, and so on. We also acted as an 'after-sales back-up support', and I went on to grow quite a large team.

Before I could get started, however, I had to spend a month at Revlon's head office learning the ropes. Thrillingly for me, the head office was in Paris!

It was time to pack my bags again.

~ 9 ~

REVLON PROFESSIONAL
(BONJOUR, PARIS)

I took the Eurostar to Paris for the first time, arriving into the Gare du Nord. I then found my way to the quaint Parisian hotel that would be my home for the next month.

The Revlon academy, where I was going to be doing my training, was on a pretty, leafy street called Rue de Paradis. It was all very exciting although, as ever, I had no idea exactly what I was letting myself in for!

After a night at the hotel, I rocked up ready for my first day at the Revlon academy. The French division had been set up by a very charming guy called Jérôme, who puffed away on countless cigarettes in his office every day. You could hardly see his desk through the fog!

Behind the scenes at the academy was very different to the 'front of house', which was all glitzy, sparkly and smart, with posters of glamorous

Revlon models. Jérôme's office, however, was just chaotic, with piles of paperwork all over the desk and on the floor. He was all very, *puff, puff, puff. Let's go out for lunch and have a glass of red wine…* They all were really.

Jérôme was married to Poucette who was about 20 years his senior, so at the time, when he was about 40 or 45, she would have been at least 60. They both became close friends of mine, and Poucette really was quite a force, with very short, spiky white hair, and a little white poodle to match! She always wore shiny, black leather trousers which looked as if they had been sprayed onto her bottom. In fact, I don't think I ever saw her wear anything else in all the years I knew her. She was such a character, spitting out her words and bossing all the other French technicians around between puffs on her cigarette.

Fortunately, everyone at Revlon in Paris spoke very good English. I was predominantly tutored by an amazing lady called Annie Enadon, who became not only a good friend, but my all-time hairdressing guru. Annie was about 10 years older than me, so around 41 or 42, and such a kind, gentle lady. At only five feet tall, she was quite petite, with shiny blonde highlighted hair.

The French team had recently started introducing Revlon products to distributors in and around Scandinavia, and Annie and another super guy called Luke invited me to be part of their team, going off to Sweden and Norway to present to the distributors, before training the salon hairdressers in how to use the products.

Very sadly, about two years after I left Paris, Annie developed lung cancer which was awful because out of everybody at the academy, she was the one who never drank or smoked, yet she succumbed; there was simply no rhyme or reason. I still can't quite believe that she passed away in her early 40s. Jérôme died a couple of years after Annie, but Poucette, who must be in her late 80s by now, is still around and living somewhere in the depths of France. Knowing her, she's probably still wearing her leather trousers and carrying a little white poodle!

I'd imagined that most of my time at the academy would be spent on learning how to use the hair relaxers and colours, but it transpired that the only technical product they had – and this is quite interesting – was a perm. It reminded me of my early days at Michael's Hair Artists, where I spent hours practising with perm rods on my poor mom's thin, uncooperative hair.

The system that Revlon Professional was still pushing out globally into the industry was called the Sensor-Perm – a perming system that used a computer. Funnily enough, Michael's Hair Artists was one of the first salon groups in England to use that system.

My month in Paris was therefore basically spent perming French ladies' hair. I couldn't help feeling that Revlon made the whole thing far more precise and complicated than it needed to be, but then I guess if you're a technician you can't cut corners and have to be able to teach the system to their exact instructions, even if you do know what you're doing.

My evenings were largely spent back in my hotel room, swatting up on all my Sensor-Perm notes, which I quite enjoyed. More than anything, I just wanted to be the best like Annie, whom I so admired.

* * *

At the end of my training, I travelled back to London and officially took up my new position with Revlon. I was given a super new company car as my job involved a lot of driving out to different salons – I usually called on three or four every day. I also ran teaching seminars: one in the morning, one in the afternoon and one in the evening, showing hairdressers how to use the Sensor-Perm system. Later, Revlon introduced their first permanent cosmetic colour line in Barcelona called Revlonissimo, a specialist product for colour technicians to use. Things then became more exciting, as we had more to offer and my training was directed more towards the colour side of things.

From the outset, I really enjoyed working for Revlon. Although I was based in the UK, there were lots of exciting opportunities for travel and, as part of the UK and Ireland Division, I would occasionally pop over to Ireland and party with the Irish hairdressers, who were always a lot of fun.

I was even asked to run a training session in a women's prison once, which was a bit weird.

The idea was to introduce the women to various vocational skills, so I was invited to host a hair colouring seminar. That was certainly a day and a half, and they were actually a super bunch of girls. I really felt for them, most of whom were in for smuggling drugs, which they'd believed they would get away with.

My main memory is of having a great day with the women, chatting with them and training them like I would with any other group, then feeling a jolt when I saw all the scissors and tail combs locked away behind glass.

When the seminar finished, I packed up all my colours and equipment and headed out to my car. I was all loaded up and about to drive off when I turned to look back at the imposing, grey stone building looming over me, and there, up in the salon, were the girls all waving down at me. I drove away thinking, *How blessed am I, that I can just jump in my car and leave…*

Working for Revlon suited me down to the ground. I loved meeting people, teaching and generally getting out and about; unfortunately, however, things weren't going so well between me and Richard. He was desperate to have children, but I just couldn't imagine us having a baby and bringing up a child in our small north London flat. Besides, I had just embarked on a new phase of my career and was really enjoying myself.

Our differing ideas about the future caused a lot of tension between us and eventually Richard decided to move out and move on. He left to go and live with a friend, leaving me alone in the flat.

It was all terribly sad, but I knew it was the right decision. I wasn't ready to be a mom. I had an amazing new career and couldn't wait to see where it would take me next. Little did I know it would be over 4000 miles away!

Jayne McCarthy

My first formal picture, aged 22, on Sun Princess

CONGRATULATIONS to Michael's Hair Artists, Telford.

Stylist: Eamonn Thatcher.

Hair coloured with Light Burgundy and Autumn Flame from the Koleston 2000 range of colours.

Dress by Wini Hemmink. Earrings by Rocks. Gloves by Denis.
136

101

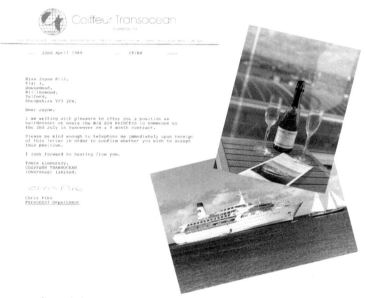

*Above left Letter from Coiffure Transocean offering me
my first job onboard ship*

Below and above: Sun Princess

PRINCESS CRUISES

SUN PRINCESS

MY HOME FOR 9 MONTHS !!
CABIN SB 41, BAJI DECK - FORWARD, PORT SIDE

*Above: A postcard home to Mom from my first voyage
on Sun Princess*

*Below: Barbados - how could I feel so alone in such a
beautiful place?*

Jayne McCarthy

Above: On my wedding day

Left and below:
The Burswood Resort Hotel and Casino

Above: My first time in Bali, with Sharon. A significant moment

Below: The very spoily Sea Goddess

Jayne McCarthy

Above: Me in a very snowy Vienna

Below: With the Revlon team in Paris

Above and below: With my guru and very special friend from Paris, Annie Enadon

PART II

~ 10 ~

THE BIG BOSS

I had been at Revlon for a couple of years when the UK and Ireland division started sharing office space with the Africa division, headed up by Nigel McCarthy. My only experience of Nigel was hearing his voice booming down the phone from the office next door when I was in a sales meeting. As far as I was concerned, he worked for a different division and wasn't on my radar. At least, that was the case until the morning I woke up in my north London flat and realised I was late for a colour technique training session in Cambridge. I jumped out of bed and into my car as fast as I could, then shot off up the M11.

I hadn't been on the road for long when my mobile phone rang. I answered to hear a familiar booming voice say, 'Good morning, Jayne. This is Nigel McCarthy...'

To say I was very surprised to get a call from 'the big boss' is an understatement. 'Good morning, Nigel,' I replied, wondering what on earth he could possibly be calling me for.

'I need some help with my division over in Nairobi and Uganda in a couple of weeks' time,' he said. 'I've had a word with your boss [a guy called Chris Threadgold] about your coming over and supporting us there for about 10 days.'

Despite being very taken aback, my immediate reply was, of course, yes! The chance to visit Africa was an offer I simply couldn't refuse, although I knew absolutely nothing about Africa. Safaris and Bob Geldof's 'Band Aid' – that was about it – but hairdressing salons? I didn't have a clue.

On the day we were due to leave, Nigel sent a taxi to pick me up from the flat and take me all the way to Gatwick airport, where we had arranged to meet. We flew with British Airways through the night to Nairobi, where Nigel wanted me to help with a big exhibition that was going on there. This was when I found myself working with black models for the first time, which meant styling black hair; something I'd never done before but fortunately I managed to wing it!

From Nairobi, Nigel and I flew to Kampala in Uganda for another big exhibition called 'Britain in Uganda', where we set up alongside various British companies, including British Gas and British Airways.

We were put up in a really smart Sheraton Hotel, along with a number of other ladies and gentlemen who were involved in the conference. Something that really caught my attention there was the behaviour of the British men. As with many big, expensive hotels in Africa, there were lots of black prostitutes in the bar, and I would sit with one of the new friends I'd made, watching the elevator going up, coming down, going up, coming down, each time with one of the British delegates that we'd shared supper with on board, and who, having clearly had a few drinks too many, would be with a black prostitute. Bearing in mind we were now at the height of the AIDs crisis, I couldn't believe how ridiculous these men were being – and how dangerous. *You might as well put a shotgun to your head, what on earth do you think you're doing?!* we'd think, shaking our heads.

After a few days in Kampala, Nigel upped and left me! 'I have to leave for Tanzania now as I've got a lot of business to do there, so can you just sort everything out here?' he said, and he literally dumped me there.

'Er... sure, okay,' I said. Once he'd gone, I thought, *Help! I've absolutely no idea what I'm doing!* It was another one of those 'feel the fear and do it anyway' situations, with me thinking, *I'm sure I'll find a way to pull this off somehow,* because that's what I do!

With Nigel gone, I managed to set up the stand and, to my credit, when he came back he seemed quite impressed with what I'd done.

On the back of that first trip to Africa, I started working regularly for Nigel's division. Initially I found visiting all the tiny salons outside Nairobi and Kampala a bit overwhelming. The staff had virtually nothing in the way of formal training and had to manage on a daily basis with the smallest amounts of shampoo, hair relaxer, or whatever it was they needed, all watered down making it less effective. A lot of the hairdressers simply made it up as they went along. Although a lack of electricity and hot water was a big problem, the passion, care and love that the people had for their work, clients and colleagues really shone through. The whole positive attitude was such a triumph over the poor amenities and rudimentary working conditions.

The more time Nigel and I spent together, the more chatty and friendly we became. There wasn't any sort of romantic spark between us during that first trip, we just worked well together and enjoyed each other's company. Nigel has an exceptional business mind, which is probably what attracted me to him in the first place – that, and his sharp suits and smart shoes. One of the strongest aspects of our relationship, once we were a couple, was always that our minds were so closely aligned when it came to work. From the beginning, I knew that I could learn a lot from him.

I returned to Africa several times as part of Nigel's technical and training team. We used to put on these really big, sparkly hair shows for Revlon's African distributors, then act as a support team once the orders came in for the products, overseeing shipment to various salons across the country.

I was soon working full time for Nigel, either with him directly, or freelancing for his division. When it came to the hair shows, I was part of a team of three, with each of us having to prepare and style 10 models for every 'performance', which was pretty tough.

Nigel and I had a lot in common when it came to business. We shared the same vision for the company and its place in Africa, and spent long and happy hours discussing all our various plans and strategies. Together we made quite the dynamic team and our becoming an 'item' felt like a natural progression of our working relationship. We decided to set up home together, finding ourselves a small house to rent just outside Kingston, which was convenient for getting to the airport, and close to Revlon's offices in Surbiton.

By 1998 we'd been in the house for a year, by which time commuting round the M25 was starting to lose its appeal. With Nigel flying all over the world – he was spending 50% of his time overseas – and me being able to work from anywhere, it dawned on us that there really wasn't a need for us to live so close to London.

So where *were* we going to live? I'd often imagined myself living in a rural idyll, somewhere deep in the countryside. Nigel agreed, so we directed our house-hunting towards Hampshire and Wiltshire; still accessible to the airport for Nigel – and me when I travelled with him – but at the same time giving me the space and tranquillity that I was starting to crave. I'd been working very hard and spending many hours in my car; now I was really taken with the idea of enjoying life in the country.

Visions of a dreamy little thatched cottage danced around in my head, as we spent our weekends house-hunting, travelling back and forth between Hampshire, Wiltshire and London. At last, after six months' searching, I saw it! The moment we stepped inside Croft Cottage, I knew I was home. We could just about afford it, with no spare cash left for furniture or decorating as such, but I didn't care, I was so incredibly excited at the prospect of this new chapter in our lives.

So what if the purchase left us broke? I didn't care – I was home!

Living at Croft Cottage suited us very well, with me dividing my time between working with Nigel in Africa, and freelancing for Revlon when I was needed. After a while, I thought it would be quite a nice idea to get to know people in Bishopstone, our local village, so I put an advert in one of the local parish magazines offering a mobile hairdressing service. It turned out to be a great idea and my client base quickly grew.

Meanwhile, Nigel was still spending two weeks out of every month overseas, either in New York or tearing around different parts of Africa. When he came home, we used to enjoy what I thought of as a 'honeymoon period'. He would arrive back at the cottage with spoily bottles of duty-free perfume and we'd wine and dine most evenings, like lovers in the first flush of romance. All too soon, however, there would be the inevitable, 'Bye, I'll see you in two weeks,' and he'd be gone again. I didn't mind. I was living in my gorgeous cottage, happily pottering around when I wasn't travelling, creating a perfect world of my own.

~ 11 ~

ESCAPE

Flushed with the success of my mobile hairdressing sideline, I had the idea of taking things to the next stage and opening my own little salon in the garden of Croft Cottage. When I mentioned the idea to my friends, most of them thought I was crazy: 'What the hell?! What on earth are you thinking?' was a common response. 'Why do you want to do that? You live right out in the sticks with no passing trade? How do you think this is going to work?'

But the more I thought about it, the more I just knew it was a good idea – more than a good idea, it was something I felt quite passionate about. 'Trust me,' I'd reply, 'because I really think this is going to work.'

I went ahead, calling my salon 'Escape', simply because that's what I wanted for my clients: escapism. Having seen some beautiful places on my travels, like the Amandari Hotel in

Bali, my mission was to create a space that was spoily and luxurious, with champagne, flowers and the client's personal choice of music playing softly in the background. There were no clocks, so the outside world, with all its time pressures, couldn't encroach on the tranquil atmosphere I worked so hard to create.

The design itself was a very personal project, and I took inspiration from some of the places I'd visited around the world. There was only space for one stylist and one client, making the whole experience bespoke and intimate.

Applying the principles of Feng Shui, the floor tiles, which I had custom-made to imitate the deck of a ship, were precision-laid so they followed a line running directly from north to south across the salon floor.

Each corner of the room had its own, very specific identity in homage to those countries around the world which had touched me in some way, or where I'd experienced a strong spiritual connection: Blue, where I washed clients' hair, symbolises water and ice, and represented Norway. Red, where I styled and cut hair, represented Africa. Here I had a striking feature mirror, designed along the lines of a wise old tree, with a base carved from a piece of cedar. Yellow was Australia, with pictures of Uluru and a tank of tropical fish. Finally, green was England, signifying my return to the Wiltshire countryside.

I was careful to provide a comfortable aesthetic, with an air-conditioning system for cooling and dehumidifying, dimmable lighting and, for an extra touch of class, I bought Philippe Starck-designed chairs, which were super comfortable and very stylish. When all the work was completed, there was even an article written about the salon in the 'Interiors' section of *Wiltshire Life*, back in September 2000.

I really had created the perfect 'Escape'!

ISABELLA
(SWEET AS PUDDING AND 'PIE')

My lovely Escape salon wasn't the only exciting thing to come along in 2000. In August 1999, Nigel and I were invited out to Las Vegas for a big hair exhibition. What a place! We attended a few business meetings, talking to suppliers and distributors in the trade and finding out about new products coming to the market; all the usual sort of thing. Then one night, much as I tried to get to sleep, I found myself tossing and turning, feeling strangely out of sorts. As I attempted to find a comfortable position, I realised that every time I moved onto my chest, it felt as if I were lying on a couple of hard, round boulders! *Whatever's wrong?!* I thought. A few days later, when I then started to feel a bit sick, it dawned on me. *I can't possibly be pregnant - can I?*

Back home at the cottage, I took a pregnancy test up to the bathroom while Nigel was in the sitting room downstairs and – boom! It was positive. I sat on the loo holding the white plastic stick, with its two, bright blue lines, thinking, *Well, that wasn't really in the plan.* Then I promptly burst into tears.

I tried to pull myself together as I headed downstairs to break the news to Nigel, still grasping on to my little plastic stick. I barely had a chance to sob out the words 'I'm pregnant' before he was smiling and laughing and cracking open the champagne!

I have to admit that it took me a little bit longer to get used to the idea of becoming a mommy. At 33, it really hadn't been on my radar, however after a couple of weeks I was every bit as thrilled as Nigel.

Our beautiful daughter was born at 6.10 pm on my 34th birthday, 9th April 2000, weighing in at 8lbs 4oz. Isabella Annie McCarthy, forever to be known affectionately as Pie (sweet as pudding and pie), was *the* best, albeit *the* most painful, birthday present ever!

Pie was placed in a tiny cot beside me in the hospital, and I was left alone in the room while

Nigel went off to phone everyone he knew and sup lots of champagne!

After a while, I dragged myself out of bed and over to the mirror. *Jesus Christ*! I thought, *Whatever do I look like?!* Staring back at me was a woman with two bleary, bloodshot eyes and wild hair, all stuck up on end. I looked like I'd been in a fight.

Quick as a flash, I got myself into the shower then set to, blow-drying my hair and putting on full makeup, including red lipstick to match my new red silk pyjamas. I finished the whole ensemble with a pair of fluffy black kitten heels.

Finally feeling a bit more like myself, I was looking down at little Pie, sleeping peacefully and completely oblivious, when a voice behind me said, 'Oh my goodness, Jayne! Are you okay?'

I turned to see the midwife staring at me in surprise. 'I'm just taking you to the maternity ward, not onto the set of *Dynasty*!' she said.

'Yes. I know that,' I replied. 'But all this helps me cope.' Which it did, not least over the next few days, as I balanced myself precariously on a bag of Tesco Finest frozen petit pois every time I sat down!

When it came to Pie's christening (a whole 10 years later!) I wrote this poem, putting into words everything I wished – and will always wish – for her future:

May you always have walls for the winds,
A roof for the rain, tea beside the fire,
Laughter to cheer you, those you love near you,
And all that your heart may desire.
May the sun shine all day long,
Everything go right, and nothing go wrong.
May those you love bring love back to you
And all the wishes you wish for, come true.
May luck always be your friend,
In whatever you do
And trouble remain a real stranger to you.
God bless x

* * *

Twelve weeks after Pie arrived, I opened my Escape salon. Looking back, I honestly don't know how I managed it – but I did! Having already worked as a mobile hairdresser, I had a really healthy client list from day one. So there I was, staggering between the cottage and the salon as I cared for my little Pie one moment, and styled hair the next.

It was a real labour of love, and I couldn't have been happier. I also couldn't have managed without the wonderful Rosemary...

~ 13 ~

ROSEMARY

Rosemary – or Rosie as Pie and I call her now – magically appeared in my life at the precise moment I needed her most, like my very own Mary Poppins. As if blown in on a wind (probably from the east), Rosemary appeared on our doorstep one dark, cold and snowy December evening in 1999, when I was five months pregnant with Pie.

It was a Saturday a few days before Christmas. Feeling more tired towards the middle of my pregnancy, I'd taken myself upstairs to bed for a nap. Meanwhile, Nigel, who was sitting by the fire in the sitting room, was surprised by a knock at the door. When he opened it, there was a local lady from the village standing there in the snow. She introduced herself as Rosemary.

Nigel invited her in, settled her in a chair by the fire in the sitting room, then came upstairs to find me.

'Jayne! Wake up!' he said. 'There's a lady downstairs who wants you to do her hair. Can you come and talk to her about it?'

'Oh for goodness' sake!' I grumbled. 'Can't you just tell her that I'm really tired and having a rest? Get her phone number and say I'll call her back next week.'

'I'm afraid I can't really do that,' Nigel replied rather sheepishly. 'She's already ensconced in front of the fire and I've just given her a glass of champagne.' This, fairly common turn of events with Nigel, left me with no choice other than to go downstairs and make myself known to our unexpected guest.

Feeling more than a little put out, I therefore staggered out of bed and dragged on my dressing gown which, unbeknown to me at the time, wasn't looking at its best with make-up marks all around the collar.

'I'm really sorry to bother you...' began Rosemary timidly, 'but...' then she launched into full throttle, 'just *look* at the state of my hair!! I can't find a good hairdresser anywhere and I've heard *so* much about you. Oh please can you do something with my hair?' And with that she was off, chatting away like there was no tomorrow. Bless Rosie, she talks a huge amount and you just can't stop her (which I know she won't mind me saying).

There was Rosemary, chat, chat, chatting away, so that within about an hour I'd heard her whole life story; from her being a manager at C&A, through her two husbands, to her children – and beyond. *Land the aeroplane Rosie,* I was thinking. *Please just get to the point!*

After a third glass of champagne, even Rosie knew it was time to brave the cold and get on her way, although not before we'd made an appointment for me to go over to her house and do her hair.

At that time, I still had no idea how important and instrumental Rosie was to become in my and Pie's lives.

A couple of weeks later, and off I went to see Rosie at her house. I was snipping away in her kitchen and we were happily chattering, Rosie reminding me about the job at C&A; the husbands and the children, when suddenly she stopped and said, 'So Jayne, are you excited to be giving up work and having your baby? I'm sure you'll really enjoy being a mommy at home.'

I paused for a second, because my mind was constantly buzzing with ideas for the exciting new salon I was creating at Croft Cottage.

'Well no, not exactly,' I said. 'Giving up work is not really the idea...' This time it was my turn to talk, as I told Rosie all about my plans for 'Escape', and how I was busy converting the dilapidated garage into a really groovy, high-end hair salon.

'At some point before the baby arrives, I'll need to go about hiring a nanny,' I said, thinking out loud as I packed away my scissors.

'Maybe,' said Rosemary carefully, 'before you advertise for a nanny, you might think of me? You know, I've looked after lots of children over many years, and I'm only around the corner. I could help you out.'

I was so surprised that I just thanked her for the very kind offer, and said that I'd think about it. It was all so out of the blue, that I hadn't really known how to respond at the time. Once Pie came along, however, and I was constantly moving back and forth between the cottage and the salon, Rosemary's childcare proposal suddenly seemed like the ideal solution.

Over the years, Rosemary has been like a second mommy to Pie, and I don't know how we would have managed without her. She's been by my side since 2000: from nappies, through school runs, all the way to Pie's graduation in Brighton. The three of us were a team – our own little family unit.

Thank you, Rosie... for everything!

~ 14 ~

OUT OF THE SLUM AND INTO THE SALON

In the years leading up to Pie's arrival, at the same time as Nigel and I were settling down to life in Wiltshire and enjoying Croft Cottage, our work continued in Africa. We attended big shows to promote Revlon's top-drawer, high-end image, talking non-stop about the colour line, perms, treatments, and whatever else was new in the glamorous world of hairdressing. However, it was becoming glaringly apparent, at least it was to us, that, first and foremost, basic hairdressing education was needed, not the showcasing and promotion of expensive new products and techniques. Proper training was required for hairdressers – particularly, and this was the bottom line – for those without the means to pay for it themselves. At that time, the few hairdressing schools that existed in Nairobi were only accessible to the rich Asian students, whose families had the means to pay the fees.

The 'Revlon East Africa Academy' was set up in downtown Nairobi in 2003, run with funding help from Revlon and 'Shair', which was a charity we created in support of the venture. Our vision, which became a reality, was to provide training for all, regardless of income.

Alongside funding from Shair (I loved that name; the coming together of sharing, caring and hairdressing), we secured sponsorship from British Airways, allowing us to fly course assessors out to the academy from the UK two or three times a year. Products were supplied by Revlon, and one of Nigel's distributors rented out the premises to us.

In between taking on mobile hairdressing clients, then opening my Escape salon, I went out to Africa five times a year, working for two or three weeks at a time, training the students. It was hard work, but I adored it and we had a lot of fun.

The students, who were very poor, walked miles and miles every day to get to their classes at the academy, leaving home at 5 am to start work at nine. It was a real learning curve – and not just for the students.

We weren't far into the project when I realised that all the toilet rolls had started disappearing. There would be a full stock at the beginning of the week, then by Wednesday the whole lot would be gone. Literally hundreds of rolls. *Whatever's happening?* I kept thinking, then I realised.

The majority of the students were female and didn't have the money to buy sanitary products. It was as simple as that. As an alternative, they were using reams of loo roll so that they could keep coming to the academy and not sit at home, which was their only other option for several days every month. Can you imagine?

Once I understood what was happening, I got together with some of the ladies who came to my salon back in Wiltshire and bought as many packs of sanitary towels and tampons as I could get in my suitcase. On my next visit to Nairobi, I took the whole lot out with me, which was great, although I was slightly concerned at the prospect of potentially having to show the contents of my case at the airport!

There were other challenges and, unfortunately, a lot of stealing of our products. It frustrated me and I used to think, *Come on guys, we're offering you everything. We're here for you, please don't do this.* Eventually, however, we just accepted that it was going to happen, and got used to it, appreciating that our students lived in the grip of a crippling poverty that was hard for us to imagine.

The academy ran for 10 years, and it really was a fun – albeit challenging – experience. We took 50 students at a time for each intensive hairdressing course, which lasted a year. At the end of the year, every student said goodbye, not only with their new qualifications, but with a bag of 'tools' for the job so they could start working straightaway. Not that anyone ever really said goodbye. The students were great at keeping in touch and letting us know, even several years down the line, what they were up to and how they were doing.

The most wonderful thing, however, was knowing that 10 years on from opening the academy, 94% of our students were still in the hair business, making a few Kenyan shillings. Our goal had never been about making money for ourselves or the company, it had been about helping people and making a difference to their lives. For me, that figure proves we were able to achieve that goal.

~ 15 ~

SECOND TIME AROUND

Opening the first hair academy in Nairobi might have been enough excitement in one year for many people – but not me. In 2003, Nigel and I decided to get married, and there's a little story I like to tell about how it all came to be…

I'm quite a spiritual person and a great believer in positive thinking, which goes hand-in-hand with ideas centred around manifestation and affirmation – if you really want something, and it's meant to be – it will come to you, provided your thoughts are positive and focussed on that goal.

Nigel and I had been thinking about getting married, although we hadn't made any firm plans as such, possibly because I didn't have a fixed idea in my mind as to what our wedding might look like. Pie was three by this time, and all I knew was that I wanted us to do something very special, just the three of us, that we would always remember, and that she would love. I had some vague ideas drifting around in the back of my mind, then, following a chance meeting, those ideas started to take shape.

It all began when a client, who was usually based in the Caribbean, happened to be visiting a cousin of hers in the village and came into my salon. While I was cutting her hair, she told me about Anguilla, the magical island paradise where she lived and managed a hotel called Cap Juluca. As she spoke, I conjured up images of turquoise waters and sugar-white sandy beaches. It was lovely just listening to her.

Before leaving the salon, she handed me a copy of the Cap Juluca brochure. I had a quick flick through, and it really did look like the most amazing dreamy place, but it was clearly a million miles out of my reach. Still, I held onto the brochure, which later found its way into the cottage and onto the kitchen table, where I'd sit down and take a little peak at the gorgeous glossy pictures every now and then, and think *Oh my God!* because it really was stunning. I also couldn't help noticing that there was a honeymoon package.

Cap Juluca had clearly always been my wedding destiny, I just hadn't realised until I saw the brochure. Nigel and I were married on the beach there with no one else around, apart from little Pie who look beautiful in a sparkly turquoise dress to match my own. It was like a photoshoot from *HELLO!* magazine – and the manifestation of a dream come true.

~ 16 ~

2ESCAPE

In 2003 I decided to do yet another crazy thing. The academy was running successfully and I thought, *We've created this amazing thing, this 'hairdresser manufacturing plant' in the middle of Nairobi, so why don't we take it a step further?* That step, I decided was to open a salon in Nairobi, staffing it with graduates from the course. I knew I was taking a risk, and, of course there were people who said I was crazy, investing so much money in Africa where there was such a different culture and outlook, not to mention managing the whole thing remotely from my cottage in Wiltshire. However, my reasoning was that if the students had worked hard to earn their qualifications, then I would offer them a career and the opportunity to leave the slum and have a real future. I was passionate about making this work and seeing what would happen.

And so 2Escape was born. Like my salon back home in Wiltshire, 2Escape represented the idea of getting away from it all; whether that meant the pressures of working and family life in the UK, or the grinding poverty of an African slum.

I've already mentioned that our students suffered a level of poverty hard to comprehend in the UK, and so on one of our trips to Nairobi, Nigel decided we needed to visit the slum at Kibera in order to gain at least some insight into how they lived and the challenges they faced.

Kibera has a population of around 200,000 and basically consists of two square miles of densely-clustered, single-storey shacks. Not only is it the largest slum in Nairobi, it's also the second largest urban slum in Africa. Nigel decided it was a place we needed to visit – and rightly so – in order to understand a little about how our students lived. Nevertheless, my overriding instinct was that I really didn't want to go, and I was quietly dreading the prospect.

The first stop on our visit was a primary school on the edge of the slum. As we walked across the main school yard, which was basically an empty area of dried mud, we saw lots of little smiley faces looking at us. The children then started jumping up and down in great excitement shouting, 'Mzungu! Mzungu!' which means 'white person' in Swahili.

Inside the school, the classrooms were small, with 48 five-to-seven-year-olds packed into one of the rooms we saw. They were all fascinated to see Pie and buzzed excitedly around her, which made her rather nervous.

Once the teacher had calmed them down and everyone was back in their seats, the children all sang 'Twinkle, Twinkle Little Star' for Pie, which was lovely – a wonderful gift from Africa's next generation.

The classroom itself was dusty and hot, especially at 2 o'clock in the afternoon, with the sun beating down on the corrugated iron roof. It was also dark, as there was no electricity. There were a few very old, beaten up little wooden desks, fewer wooden chairs and a single, lonely torn poster on the wall setting out the numbers from one to 10 in different colours.

At the end of the visit, we thanked all the children and their teacher as we said our goodbyes. Once we were outside again and our eyes began to adjust to the strong, bright sunlight, Pie quietly said, 'Where is the colour in the classroom, Mumma? Why didn't they have any books?'

From the school, we moved further into the heart of the slum, and a world that felt completely alien. It's hard to describe, and all I can say is that it felt like being in the biggest maze you could ever imagine. The smell, more than anything else, really assaulted my senses. It was like a barbeque in a hot, dirty toilet, with raw waste carving gullies along the ribbons of bare earth that served the streets and alleyways. Forests of twisted ariels sprouted from the roofs of the shacks, and all around us children crawled and played in dirt that you wouldn't even step in, unless it was impossible to avoid

The main streets were full of hustle and bustle. Airtel and M-Pesa billboards competed with signs for the butcher's, charcoal sellers and hair salons. The barrage of colour was overwhelming, and somehow at odds with the stifling, awful smell. Everything conspired to make me feel uncomfortable, like a sneaky intruder embarrassed by my privileged ignorance. Thankfully, I seemed to be invisible amid the busyness of this huge, throbbing community.

Don't get emotional, don't you dare cry, I kept repeating to myself. *Keep walking, head held high. Walk with purpose. Smile and say hello…*

I noticed hundreds of tiny salons as we walked around, and at one called 'Turning Point', which I thought was an interesting name, I stopped to chat with two of the girls who worked there. Their names were Millicent and Sarah, both of whom later came to work with me at 2Escape.

We visited several salons, where it was invariably the case that the products were watered down to make them last longer, which was a shame because it meant nothing produced the right results, or was as effective as it should have been. Clients would sometimes bring their own products to be used in the salon, with many bringing braids which, being the cheapest option for hair styling, were very popular.

As we carried on walking, I noticed a ribbon of dirty pink net curtain fluttering innocently on the hot breeze. This was in the doorway to another salon called 'Salon Afrique', with the byline 'Looking Good Salon' helpfully added underneath. I put my head inside and called out, 'Jambo!' which is 'Hi' in Swahili. Inside was a very smiley stylist who introduced herself as Boniface. Clearly the 'momma' of the salon, she had been attending to her second client of the day, a shampoo and set, when we arrived.

Inside, the salon was very small and dimly lit, with tired old empty product bottles littering the wooden shelves, and a cracked mirror hanging from a loose nail. I noticed that the client looked rather nervous as she sat on a rickety white plastic chair.

By the end of our slum visit, I couldn't help but admire everyone we saw and spoke to. These people have so very little, but still try with all their might to make some kind of living; keeping going day after day and night after long, noisy night. There's no planning and no thought for tomorrow, all their efforts go into surviving today. Without any government aid, benefits or national health care system to support them, the only things they can rely on are each other and their faith.

* * *

Plans for the 2Escape salon all came together very well and it was up and running successfully. Then, in 2007, a series of post-election riots brought turmoil to Kenya. It was horrendous, with looting and bloodshed that resulted in us having to close the salon and everyone being told to stay at home.

I telephoned my six members of staff every day to check they were okay. Then the inevitable day came, just before New Year's Eve, when I couldn't get hold of one of them; a lovely guy called Cornelius. It was terribly worrying, not least because I was completely powerless to do anything.

Eventually, on New Year's Day, Cornelius managed to call me from the salon where he was standing in rags, absolutely destitute with nothing. He told me the horrific story of how, a few days earlier, three rioters had broken into his shack in the slum armed with machetes, beaten him up and beheaded a friend of his, who had been staying with him. Mercifully, Cornelius' wife and sons were away, living in Mombasa.

At around this time, I'd been considering opening another salon called 2Escape2, this time in Mombasa, with Cornelius as the manager. He'd worked so hard at 2Escape and really was the star of the show there, despite not being in charge. I'd always told him that the next salon would be his, so once I'd returned to Kenya, secured the premises for the new 2Escape2 and sorted out all the details, I met up with Cornelius and said, 'Can I take you home to Mombasa?'

He was overjoyed, jumping up in excitement and sending his glass of wine one way and his napkin the other! 'You've made every dream I've ever had come true,' he said.

I wish that had been the happily ever after to end the story, but sadly – and we're talking about Africa, after all – things didn't all run according to plan. A year after the election riots in Nairobi, I received a phone call from Hilton, the manager at 2Escape, telling me there had been an armed raid at the salon. 'Everyone is fine,' he said, but of course the whole thing was very shocking and not the news I'd wanted to hear.

It transpired that Cornelius had been the real lynchpin at 2Escape and, despite not being the manager in charge, had effectively run the place. With him now running 2Escape2 in Mombasa, it was clear that Hilton was out of his depth and couldn't cope. Add a few 'rotten apples' into the mix, and the venture had started to come apart at the seams.

It was really difficult news for me to take in. I hadn't been creating these salons for profit, they were purely – literally – a means of escape, and had the potential to be a real change in fortune for our ex-students whom I so passionately wanted to help. I certainly learned a lot from the whole venture, and whilst I wasn't put off, it made me understand the huge importance of having the right team on board.

The problem I was always going to face in Africa was the poverty. These guys lived lives of unrelenting penury and, for them, the whole concept of working hard today in order to reap the rewards tomorrow, was a fantasy they couldn't afford to believe in.

* * *

After many adventures, dramas, and heartfelt stories – including opening a second academy in Kigali – our African tales came to an end. It became increasingly difficult to manage the salons and academies remotely, with our being 5,000 miles away back in Wiltshire most of the time. But… what a time we had! It was a true gift to have been able to help educate so many in the skill of hairdressing.

Happy hair days, you beautiful people!

Jayne McCarthy

Croft Cottage in summer and winter

Wiltshire Life article on the opening of my 'Escape' salon

INTERIORS BY JUDE MULHERN

Travel around the world while getting your hair cut.

I LOVE going to the hairdressers. Usually I arrive in a foul mood having battled for a space in the multi-storey car park, and then fought my way through frenzied shoppers. I start to relax when I am being shampooed and by the time I hear that sensual snip of scissors cutting hair and see my wild mop being encouraged into something vaguely resembling a style, I'm in heaven!

The pleasure though, is more often than not marginalised by the jarring sounds of the current teen pop band competing with the client in the next chair, twittering on about her boyfriend problems. What I want is total relaxation; so what a joy to discover that there is now a salon in Wiltshire that embraces this concept.

At Escape in Bishopstone not only will you be the sole client getting undivided attention and unlimited pampering, but you can also enjoy the beautiful and innovative interior and a selection of harmonious sounds.

When Jayne Lowe and husband Nigel decided to convert their garage into a hairdressing salon they were determined to create something original. Jayne has travelled extensively during her career, which includes working as a

technical specialist for Revlon Professional and manageress on board luxury cruise liners.

She wanted the salon interior to reflect the path of her career to date and decided that the walls would be painted using the whole colour spectrum. Not an easy task, but by a process of trial and error using 17 different paints with both wet and dry rollers, an amazing effect has been achieved.

The four corners of the room each have their own identity, and as Jayne wanted to incorporate some of the principles of Fung Shui (the Chinese geomancer's art of divining harmony between nature and mankind) into her design she made sure that the north (water) corner was blue and the south corner red. The floor tiles are laid on the north to south diagonal and resemble faded planks of wood as on the deck of a ship. The skirting is tiled using the same material, and the edge finished with a natural rope.

Each of the four corners of the room, every one in a different colour, represent a country Jayne has worked in; the blue corner is Norway and has images of water and ice, which is also the area where hair is washed. The red corner is Africa and this is where hair is styled.

Clients sit in front of a feature mirror based on a contemporary design of a wise old tree. The base was carved from a piece of cedar, and the branches and leaves that form the mirror frame are made of wrought iron. The yellow corner is Australia and is completed with photographs of Ayers Rock and a tank of tropical fish. Finally there is the west corner which is green and signifies the return to Wiltshire.

Abstract photographs of the countries were found in a local photographers' image library, printed and framed. Jayne and Nigel gave careful consideration to both the aesthetic and practical aspects of this project; an air conditioning system that is for cooling, dehumidifying and heating has been installed so that the temperature can be properly controlled.

The state-of-the-art stereo system has speakers recessed in the ceiling, a neat space saving solution. The lighting system is a combination of small chrome directional downlights and plaster wall uplighters painted to match the walls. All the lights are on dimmers so the atmosphere can be changed at the flick of

FACT FILE

Paints – Dulux from B&Q, Salisbury 01722 332299
Floor Tiles – Tiles R Us 01722 416131
Wrought Ironwork – John Edmunds 01722 781212
Plaster Wall Uplighters – The Lighting Workshop 01722 326895
Chairs – Philippe Starck Distribution Company, Paris
Paris Framed Photographs – Haywards 01722 340394
Jude Mulhern is available for interior design consultation on 01722 336963

a switch and a corner picked out as appropriate.

The sleek grey chairs are all from a range designed by the renowned Philippe Starck and are as comfortable as they are stylish. The success of this interior is in the attention to detail; the salon has a fresh contemporary feel and is the perfect place to unwind as Jayne works wonders with your hair.

• *Escape – for hairdressing, Indian head massage, manicure and pedicure. Phone for appointment 01722 780116.*
• *Do you have a beautiful home or interior we could feature in Wiltshire Life? Contact the editorial office: the address is on the contents page.*

Top: Hair styled in Africa.
Above: Get a shampoo in Norway

Jayne McCarthy

In my newly opened 'Escape' salon in Wiltshire

For the ultimate salon experience...

The DREAM...

Relaxation in tranquil surroundings

Stir the senses

Massage the soul

One Client

One Stylist

One Vision

The perfect salon environment

The REALITY...

Relaxation in tranquil surroundings

Stir the senses

Massage the soul

One Client

One Stylist

One Vision

The perfect salon environment

Indian head massage is a deeply relaxing and therapeutic massage treatment for the upper back, shoulders, neck, scalp and face. It helps relieve tense and stiff muscles, promotes hair condition and growth and aids lymphatic drainage, ridding the body of toxins.

Enjoy 35 minutes of pure relaxation with a treatment that will assist in lifting you away from the stresses of daily life to help recharge and re-energise your mind and body.

Jayne McCarthy

Escape with Jayne Lowe - your personal hair technician...

Jayne has a wealth of experience which extends to over 20 years within the hairdressing industry. Her wide and varied career has taken her around the world. Positions held include manageress on-board luxury cruise liners, Style Director at Harrods in London and UK Technical Specialist for Revlon Professional, which included the teaching and training of hairstylists.

Jayne welcomes you to Escape, where you can be assured of receiving the very best care, service and advice for every aspect of your haircare.

To Escape call 01722 780116
By appointment only
Monday to Friday 10am to 6pm

escape

160

Isabella - Sweet as Pudding and 'Pie'

Jayne McCarthy

Above: With Pie on holiday in Spain

Below: Pie on her first trip to Africa

With Pie on holiday

Jayne McCarthy

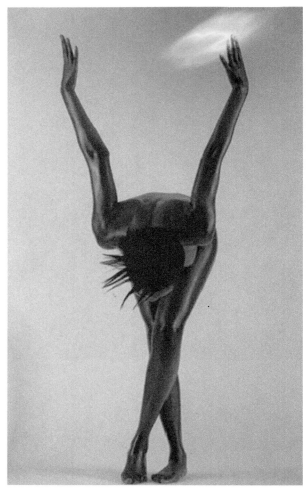

Photograph: 'Salutations'
This image epitomises my work in Africa

Headline and image from an article on the
Revlon East Africa Academy in Nairobi

PART III

~ 17 ~

THE BRAZILIAN BLOW-OUT

I couldn't write my story and not talk about some of the very special people who have come into my life, one of whom is Brazilian hairdresser Gilles Gonçalves, an influential hairstylist who was at the very top of his game when our paths crossed in 2010.

I first saw the name Gilles Gonçalves when I read the glossy magazines like *Vogue* and *Harpers & Queen*. He was much written-about as the hairdresser who pioneered an amazing new treatment called the 'Brazilian blow dry' – a semi-permanent technique for straightening frizzy, unmanageable hair using keratin. I just thought, *Gosh, I really need that treatment for my clients in my little tucked-away Wiltshire salon.*

After a bit of research, I managed to track Gilles down and I called him at his salon. We had a really nice conversation and when I told him that I was very interested in his Brazilian blow-drying technique, he said, 'Where exactly are you, Jayne? Why don't I come and visit you on Sunday? I can see your salon set-up and teach you how to do it.'

I told Gilles that would be wonderful and we agreed that I would collect him from the station at Salisbury the following Sunday. It wasn't until I put the phone down and dug a bit deeper into Gilles on the internet that I saw what a huge name he was in the hairdressing world, with a clientele list that included Kylie Minogue, Rhianna and Gwyneth Paltrow, to name just a few. *Oh my God,* I thought, *how can this big, big celebrity hairdresser say that he wants to give up his Sunday, get on the train, leave London and come and see me in the Wiltshire countryside?*

Gilles told me that for him to demonstrate the Brazilian blow dry at its best, I needed to find a model who had the frizziest, fluffiest, curliest and most out-of-control hair that I could think of. Luckily, my friend Jillie fitted the bill perfectly. On that Sunday, not only did Gilles totally transform Jillie's hair, but our wonderful friendship began.

And there was far more to come… because two years later I had a call from Gilles. 'Oh my God,' he said, 'I've just had a call from a client of mine, Lady X – she's the wife of a "famous business mogul", and she wants me to put together a team of hairdressers and make-up artists and fly them out to Cancun in Mexico for her husband's 60th birthday!'

Gilles wanted me to be part of that team, which was incredibly exciting. It was also a very timely opportunity for me as my mom had recently died and, having found myself stuck in a dark, sad place, the idea of a new adventure gave me a much-needed lift. Although I have to say, the clientele list was very intimidating, and I was really quite nervous!

The birthday celebrations organised by Lady X involved a week of full-blown partying for around 160 guests, all of whom were flown by private jet to an exclusive resort near Cancun, with the staff staying at a hotel nearby. As I boarded the plane at Heathrow, I looked around me and thought, *Crikey, some of the best hairdressers and makeup artists in the world are here, but I've no idea who they are or where they are.* I just hoped that I would be able to pull it off – but then I told myself, as I always do, *Feel the fear but do it anyway!*

In terms of support crew, there were 450 of us in total, working on hair, beauty, fireworks, catering and lots more. A big events company based in London called Banana Split was overseeing the whole thing. Their philosophy was *If you can dream it, we can create it!* And they did.

Our job was to look after the ladies' hair; putting it up, blow drying or doing whatever else we might have been asked, ahead of the main events which were three themed parties on three different nights.

We set up our salon and spent a lot of time travelling between our hotel and the luxury guest resort. Apparently, the budget for the week's partying was in the region of £6m so, as you can imagine, the whole event was quite surreal! There were so many celebrities wafting around, but the one guest I was really interested in meeting was Simon Cowell, as I'd always rather liked him. *Right,* I thought to myself, *at some point during the week I'm going to meet Mr Cowell. Who knows, maybe I'll even cut his hair?!*

The first party on the Monday night had a 'White and Diamonds' theme, which was all very glamorous. Then on the Wednesday, which was Sir X's birthday night, the theme was 'Spanish Flamenco'. More than anything else that week, this party really was incredible. Lady X had hired top scene designers to create a Spanish ambience, and with each invitation she sent out came a request for the guest's clothes and shoe size so she could individually create every single outfit.

There were, in the dressing rooms, surrounded by tables lined with different coloured jewels, makeup and all the trimmings you could imagine. Lady X had stressed that each person had to have their makeup and hair done in accordance with her particular instructions with no variations – she really was very strict.

Once we'd completed the hair and makeup, the guests were shipped off to the party in gorgeous gold carriages, pulled by immaculately groomed white ponies. It felt as if we were creating a film set and the whole thing really was quite extraordinary, right down to Stevie Wonder turning up to sing 'Happy Birthday to You'. It was mad!

The final party was for Sir and Lady X's daughter, who was, let's just say, a bit tricky. It was her 21st birthday and Banana Split had created this huge, magical wooden venue on the beach with multicolour lasers criss-crossing the sky and thousands of pounds' worth of fireworks to kick things off.

We did everybody's hair and makeup during the afternoon then, ahead of the party, Lady X came to see us and said, 'Guys, you've done such an amazing job, you're all invited to my daughter's birthday party, just don't arrive before midnight.'

As soon as we'd finished with our last clients, we shot back to the hotel where we excitedly had our first glass of champagne of the week which was, of course, pink Cristal. Once we were all dressed up and ready to go, we headed off to the beach where a huge oak door stood at the entrance to the venue.

It was like entering a fairy tale. We walked down a long corridor all bathed in candlelight and adorned with tropical flowers. As we moved through, marvelling at the scenery and all the work Banana Split had put into everything, we could hear the DJ playing Robbie Williams' 'Rock DJ' and decided the first thing to do was to hit the dance floor.

We opened the door and suddenly all the lighting was fluorescent pink and it wasn't a Robbie Williams *track* playing, it was actually Robbie Williams himself! Can you imagine?! He was there, right in front of us singing 'Rock DJ'.

At around 2 am, with everyone still partying away and having a marvellous time, I suddenly spotted Simon Cowell sitting across the other side of the dance floor, talking to a Russian billionaire. *Okay…* I thought, *this is your moment. If you don't go and say hello, you'll regret it.*

Off I went, imagining myself to be smoothly slinking across the dance floor in my sparkly cocktail dress. In a real 'fan girl' moment, I plucked up the courage and tapped him on the shoulder. 'I'm sorry to interrupt,' I said, looming over Simon Cowell, 'but I've always wanted to meet you – hello.'

He looked up at me with his polished, Botoxed face, smiled his bluey-white Hollywood smile, and stood to talk to me and – this is the funniest thing – he was on his feet but I was still looming over him. I hadn't realised quite how short he was. *Oh gosh, that's a bit weird!* I thought. Despite being somewhat vertically challenged, he was very polite and I managed to have a nice conversation with him.

All in all, it was an amazing night. Naomi Campbell in particular sticks in my mind as she looked like the most beautiful black swan, swimming around in a sea of glittering famous faces. I styled the hair of lots of celebrities, including Gwyneth Paltrow (lovely and very down to earth); Kate Moss (basically on her phone the whole time); Kate Hudson (again, lovely) and even Leonardo di Caprio's mother (another super lady).

However, there's 'always one' as they say, and a certain very glamorous television presenter arrived with her trademark long, thick hair… in a plastic bag! She then proceeded to give me very strict instructions as to how these extensions should be woven into her own, rather thin hair. She was a bit of a 'diva' about the whole thing!

On the Friday lunchtime we were allowed to hang out at the infinity pool with the celebrities, on the proviso that we remained at a respectable distance from their antics, as they paraded about in their sparkly bikinis and Jimmy Choo sandals. It was such fun to watch them. They'd be eating their lobster one minute, and the next Bruno Mars might appear with his band and start playing, or Ronnie Wood would jump up and do an incredible dive into the pool. It was like being in a crazy movie.

I really did have the most amazing week; the Daily Mail even covered the event and I still have the cuttings. As crew, we were fortunate in that our working hours boiled down to just 12, spread across four afternoons. We were paid £800 a day, and spent most of our time pottering around by the swimming pool.

It was a great experience and such a contrast to the work I'd been doing in the slums of Africa. I had gone from mixing with the poorest of the poor, to the richest of the rich, which of course gave rise to an element of discomfort, like knowing the burgers at the beach barbeque were made from Japanese Wagyu beef, one of the most expensive cuts of meat in the world with each burger costing about £50.

Gilles and I remained good friends and he still styles Lady X's hair to this day. Every eight weeks she flies him to Monaco by private jet – she spends a lot of time on her yacht there – where he de-glues her old hair extensions and puts in new ones. He charges her £3,000 a visit, and on top of which he gets a £500 tip and a few glasses of champagne, before being flown back to London.

Despite all the luxury, Gilles is a wonderfully down-to-earth character. He once said to me, 'Jayne, I can't believe it. How did this happen?' He came from a very, very poor family in São Paulo before moving to London and becoming a hairdresser. 'How is it that now, the money from one client can more than cover my mortgage?!' he said.

Gilles was keen to learn more about my work in Africa and so, a couple of years after the event in Mexico, we travelled there together. I showed him the main slum at Kibera, where he saw dozens of small shacks with corrugated iron roofs and barely any water or electricity. At one point, he spotted a barber's shop. 'I'm going to get my hair cut here,' he announced.

'Gilles!' I said, surprised, 'you probably shouldn't. They tend to use rusty scissors and their clippers are always very worn out.' But he was determined and afterwards told me that it was probably the best haircut he'd ever had. It cost him the equivalent of 75p.

~ 18 ~

DEBORAH

Deborah Rodriguez is another friend who has played an important part in my life. I first came to know her back in 2015, when I was married to Nigel and living and working in our cottage in Wiltshire.

I discovered Deborah – indirectly – when a regular client of mine, an American lady called Julie, came in for a haircut one morning.

'Jayne,' she said, as she took her coat off and settled into the chair, 'I've just spent the last hour in Waterstones in Salisbury choosing a few new books. I saw this one and thought of you. Here you go, it's a present.' She handed me a book called *The Kabul Beauty School,* a memoir by a lady called Deborah Rodriguez.

'Oh, thanks. That's kind,' I said, rather doubtfully, thinking, *Oh no, she's coming again in six weeks so I'm going to have to make a real effort to read this book, otherwise it will seem very ungrateful.*

I dutifully started reading *The Kabul Beauty School* that night and before long it hit me that Deborah was basically writing my own story. In her memoir, which had only been out for a year or so, she describes working as a hairdresser in America before deciding to go off to Afghanistan and set up an academy in Kabul. Her aim was to train Afghan women in hairdressing skills so they would have the freedom to live independently and earn their own money.

Reading Deborah's book was fascinating: the heat, the dust, the potholes everywhere, and the generators that kept breaking down, not to mention fighting for sponsorship for hair products, then working hard to get them shipped in. There were so many difficulties and dramas, and all the time I was thinking, *This is the weirdest thing… this is like me! I could have written this book,* because when she was setting up her academy in Kabul, I was doing exactly the same in Nairobi. When I reached the end of the book, I knew that I had to find Deborah and talk to her.

It was October when I started doing some internet research on her using my iPad, tucked away in my den – a cosy log cabin under the willow tree at the side of the cottage, all lit with candles. I found Deborah on Facebook and decided to send her a very short message:

Hi Deborah,

I just wanted to say how much I enjoyed The Kabul Beauty School. *It's funny really, because reading your book felt as if I was following you. I've been doing exactly the same thing as you, but in Africa.*

Thank you for your wonderful story,
Jayne

In reality, I honestly hadn't expected to hear back from her, so when I received a message literally five minutes later, I was amazed:

Hey Jayne,

That's so kind of you, thank you. Tell me more about Africa…

181

We corresponded over Messenger for a couple of days, telling each other what we were up to and the things we'd done in the past. I wrote:

Hi Deborah,

Where are you now? Are you still in Afghanistan?'

Deborah replied that she wasn't in Afghanistan any longer but that, having gone back to America briefly, she knew there was no way she could live there any longer.

Hi Jayne,

I now live in Mexico. It's a little place you won't have heard of on the west coast called Mazatlán.

Mazatlán! I thought, *What are the chances?!*

Hi Deborah,

I do know Mazatlán! I don't suppose that mad, crazy restaurant/bar called Senior Frogs is still there, is it?'

Deborah confirmed that Senior Frogs was indeed still there, and just around the corner from Tippy Toes, her salon where she trains disadvantaged women in Mexico.

Hi Deborah,

Wow! Maybe, just maybe, one day I'll meet you in Senior Frogs and we can share our hair stories together.

Hi Jayne,

How about November? That would be perfect.

Oh my God! I couldn't believe it. By now we'd been chatting for about a month, although only ever on Messenger. Somehow, though, I felt as if our meeting was just meant to be. I had this strong feeling that I really wanted to see her, not least because she almost sounded like another me and – of course – she does hair!

Hoping that I had accumulated a few air miles from all my toing and froing to Africa, I phoned British Airways to ask if they could get me to Mazatlán. I spoke to this really helpful guy who told me there were flights available, leaving from Heathrow to Mexico City, then connecting to Mazatlán. As he was talking me through the itinerary he said, 'Oh, this could be quite nice for you Jayne… we can fly you there and back first class.'

That sealed it for me. I messaged Deborah and told her it was all arranged and I was coming to Mazatlán. 'That's amazing,' she replied. 'You'll be here with me for Thanksgiving which is a big thing for us.'

So off I went on another adventure, flying out to a tiny town in Mexico that I'd last visited 30 years previously, to meet a woman whom I'd never met in person before, and whose voice I'd never actually heard.

* * *

I gazed out of the plane window as we made a very clattery, very bumpy landing into Mazatlán at one o'clock on the Monday morning. As we bounced down onto the tarmac, I was feeling nervous and excited, as well as tired and slightly anxious, wondering exactly what the next few days would have in store. When I looked out of the window, however, there, right in front of my bleary eyes amidst the darkness and twinkling lights, was the brightest, most magical shooting star bursting across the sky.

Next morning, Deborah and her partner Dennis arrived to meet me at my hotel at 10.30 am. The plan had been for us to meet at nine, but then I thought *Hey, it's like Africa here with the same, slightly 'mañana' approach to life.* I remembered Dennis from her book, *Carnival Street,* which I'd been furiously reading during my spoily British Airways first class flight. The book is named after the street where she and Dennis live in Mazatlán.

They greeted me very warmly, with Deborah announcing that we needed to visit Tippy Toes before we did anything else as she had a few 'hair issues!'

The salon, like my hotel, has a rather glamorised website! It is lovely though; quite small and cosy, situated down a quiet, potholed, dusty side street. The interior is a mix of a typical American 'shabby chic' salon, crossed with an African, slightly cluttered, chaotic set-up. Still, I decided it worked, and worked very well.

It was very busy when we arrived, mainly with the ex-pat brigade. Deborah calls them the 'snowbirds' because they fly down from America and Canada for the winter season. Her Mexican staff were furiously soaking, filing and painting all shapes and sizes of feet, toes, hands and fingernails. Not that they needed to rush as all the clients seemed set for the day, armed with the latest romantic novels, multi-coloured knitting and scandalous gossip. I even noted a Shisha pipe beside the backwashes, nestled between the Paul Mitchell shampoos: *That's strange,* I thought. Overall, the atmosphere was alive, noisy and fun.

I felt like the big celebrity when Deborah introduced me to everyone as 'Jayne, the English hairdresser who read my book and decided to come to Mexico and say "Hi".' She also told everyone that despite us only ever communicating by text until today, we'd both known that we were destined to meet.

Being introduced to Deborah's salon 'family' in person was quite a surreal experience, not least because they are all characters in her book. It was like entering the set of a film adaptation of one of her novels. I already knew many of the characters' individual stories, often tales of the sadness and hardship they had endured before Deborah came to the rescue, throwing out a lifeline of love, care and hope within Tippy Toes.

It was something I understood very well from my salons in Kenya.

Then, of course, there was the 'hair issue' that had necessitated us hot-footing it over to Tippy Toes that morning. Apparently, Martha, a very attractive young member of staff with the most beautiful chocolate brown eyes I'd ever seen, had spent 10 hours working on Deborah's hair the day before, bonding in a mixture of blonde, copper and red hair extensions. Deborah told me it had all been going quite well until, somewhat understandably, Martha had become teary and lost interest, needing a sit down and a rather large Tequila! Which is how *my* skills came to be put to the test after just a handful of minutes in a totally alien Mexican salon, as Deborah asked me to complete her new look. Whilst she was happy with half a head of real Russian hair, she explained that that shape just wasn't working.

I took a deep breath and plunged in, as I always do when faced with a challenge that I've no idea how the hell to tackle. I started sculpting, addressing the somewhat unruly glued-in tufts, which was tricky since tools for the job were rather scarce. When I asked for a razor to thin out the clumps, Deborah produced a disposable Bic from her red Gucci handbag. 'I tidied up my legs with it this morning,' she said, 'but it still has plenty of bite left.' Absolutely hilarious, and definitely a first for me! It worked though, and Deborah was thrilled – thank the Lord!

Dennis then strolled back into the salon – such a gentle, relaxed chap – and announced it was time for the 'English rose' to sample her first Margarita of the week. *Yes*, I thought, *I could do with that after passing my first Deborah Rodriguez hair test*.

The three of us set off, trotting down the road to Macaws Bar and Restaurant. This fun and buzzy place features many times in one of Deborah's books and, when she was new to Mazatlán, it was her number one haunt for making friends. At Macaws I was introduced to Alicia, the top cocktail waitress, a super-attractive, size-zero senorita with the largest boob enhancement known to man, or woman for that matter! My margarita was truly the best I'd ever tasted.

While Dennis supped on ice cold Coronas, Deborah popped off to the liquor store to purchase a spoily bottle of red wine. 'You can't trust the local bars,' she said, 'their wine is usually shit!' which made me laugh. She really is such an entertaining, funny and wonderful lady, and we felt as if we'd known each other forever, with chat and giggles flowing freely. We spent the rest of the day nibbling on tacos, guacamole and herby broiled fish while we shared all our hair stories.

The next day, Deborah and Dennis picked me up from my hotel and we set off to Angelina's, apparently the hottest place in town for breakfast, where we were joined by three American friends of Deborah's. They were all very jolly – and rather noisy, given the time of day! – chatting about the amazing and handsome 'new-in-town' Botox doctor; what to do about the terribly unreliable Mexican dog groomer; and how on earth could Bill, their shared gardener, have picked up a flesh-eating virus? They then went into explicit detail about how his flanks were looking, by which point I nearly up-chucked my chopped, fried chorizo. Not and ideal start to the day!

We arrived at Tippy Toes to find all the staff busily sprucing the place up, ready for the next batch of cruise ship clients due that day. I found it funny to think that, years ago, it was me working on a cruise ship and heading off to Senior Frogs with my fellow crew members, where we got absolutely hammered on margaritas and danced in our sparkly bikinis on the tables.

It was clearly going to be a busy day in the salon and almost at once, Dolores from Texas and Mary from Michigan made an entrance; rather large American old dears dressed in matching attire which consisted of baggy white knee length shorts and alarmingly tight, pink fluorescent t-shirts embossed with the cruise ship's name. Maybe the onboard boutique had run out of their XXXL sizes?!

Meanwhile Deborah was busy on her mobile phone chatting to a friend about their plans for Thanksgiving night, while the dusty old radio in the corner of the salon vibrated, seemingly having a panic attack, as it reported the news that a hurricane was supposedly due to hit us that same night. I could hear Deborah saying she was concerned that the caterers might not be able to deliver the feast she had ordered for the evening, while I was fretting that we'd all be blown away – never mind the turkey and pecan pie.

Deborah gave me the nod to get cracking with Dolores and Mary. I'd been quietly assessing the cruise ship queens' hair and, true to form, there was no change from the American oldies I'd styled 24 years ago. Looking at Mary, it was my guess that she had at least three perms and four, full-head permanent colours, torturing her fine, frail hair.

Dolores, who displayed a real life 'trick-or-treat Halloween' hairdo, wedged her ample bottom into the chair, which I worried might stay put when she waddled over to the backwash!

'You talk real cute,' she said in her squeaky southern drawl. 'You wanna give my bangs the once over?'

'Certainly,' I replied, doing a quick translation and remembering that 'bangs' meant 'fringe'.

'I need you to tease me real hard today,' she demanded, a phrase I hadn't heard since my days on the cruise ships many years before.

Dolores managed to extract herself from the groaning chair and I escorted her over to the backwash, '… and *no* conditioner,' she added, something else I'd heard many-a-time from those elderly American ladies all those years ago. *Yeah, okay,* I thought, *but how am I going to comb my way through this bag of nails without conditioner?*

From past experience I knew to say nothing, then quietly add a few drops of detangling spray on her matted mane as she nattered loudly to Mary about the crappy onboard entertainment.

I began blow drying while Dolores and Mary chattered away about their time on the cruise ship. 'What time did they say the midnight buffet was?' asked Dolores. *Unbelievable!* I thought, remembering how the Americans used to ask me this day in and day out when I was on board. *What is it with some Americans, I think they pack everything in their suitcase apart from their brains when going on vacation?* Feeling naughty I replied, 'When I worked at sea, the midnight buffet was always at 10.30 pm.'

'Gee, thanks for that honey,' said Mary.

Coiffured and set with cans of hairspray and notorious amounts of teasing, Dolores and Mary seemed very happy with their hairdos. 'You give a *real swell* shampoo,' Mary said, then asked me if I'd seen her shiny pink fanny bag! Quick translation again, *Oh yeah, that means bum bag*. If I hadn't picked up on that years ago, I would have been wondering what on earth that fanny bag was concealing – the mind boggles!

Later, Deborah announced that it was time for me to have a treat, 'There ain't no way you can travel all the way from London and not have a pedicure at Tippy Toes,' she declared, clicking her fingers and summoning Alex, the top toe dude.

Alex, a small, chubby, 19-year-old Mexican, minced over in his super-tight faded jeans and linen white shirt, preening his bleached white Mohican hair in the mirror as he went. He frowned as I sat down, clearly assessing the intense, industrial work required to rejuvenate my tired, swollen, hard-skinned feet and raggedy, discoloured toe nails.

On the plane over, I had promised myself that I would learn a few Spanish words, so when Alex's eyes met mine over his torturous task, I was able to mutter, 'Lo siento, mi amigo,' which literally translates to, 'I'm sorry, my friend.'

An hour and a half later, I was walking on air as I admired my super, glossy pink toes. Alex was also smiling, thanks to the generous tip I gave him.

For the next few days, Deborah and I walked, talked, sipped on margaritas and just lived in the moment, knowing they were precious and rapidly closing in on us.

'Are you ready to hit the pit?' Deborah asked wearily on our last night together at Angelina's.

'Yes, sadly I think I am,' I said, as we headed back to my hotel.

When we pulled up, Deborah parked the car and switched off the ignition. We sat quietly in the darkness for a while, looking out at the gloriously moonlit beach and the sparkling waves.

'You know, I can't quite believe we've only been together for a week, Jayne,' she said at last. 'It feels as if you've been in my life forever!

I don't know what we are destined for but I feel it is something great and fun. We are going to be together for the rest of our lives.'

'Absolutely,' I replied sleepily.

We hugged one another and I stepped out of the car.

'Until next time,' said Deborah.

'Until next time…'

As it turned out, next time came sooner than I imagined and, just a year after our trip to Mazatlán, I received a call from a very excited Deborah.

'I'm researching a new book and we need to go to Zanzibar,' she said. 'We have to find out about witch doctors, voodoo, spices and magic… I've got a list!'

'We?' I said.

'I need a research assistant,' she replied. 'Do you want to come with me?'

Sure. Why the hell not? I thought, never being one to turn down the chance of a new adventure… which our trip certainly proved to be!

ZANZIBAR
(THE SPICE ISLAND)

Deborah's 'work in progress' was a novel called *The Zanzibar Wife*, and in order to get 'under the skin' of the story and really bring it to life, she wanted to visit Zanzibar to absorb the atmosphere and glean information as much as she could about the people and their way of life.

'Of course I'll come with you!' I said. I was very flattered that she wanted to bring me along on her journey and, as you know, I never turn down an opportunity to travel somewhere new.

Deborah planned the whole trip, visiting various travel agents who – apparently – all told her that under no circumstances should two middle-aged Western women, travelling alone, stay in Stone Town, which is the centre of the city.

'Obviously we're not going to listen to them,' she said, when relaying this all back to me. 'We need to stay down town so we can get right into the heart of the place; down to the bones of the island.'

'Sure, okay,' I said. I wasn't surprised at her response, but felt rather shaky nevertheless. Still, I managed to hold my nerve.

We arranged to meet in Nairobi ahead of our trip, where we stayed overnight before setting off for Zanzibar, the magical spice island!

When we finally arrived in Stone Town, it was to a gorgeous boutique, Arabic-style family-run hotel in the traditional style, with vast, beautifully carved wooden doors. Deborah and I shared a huge bedroom with a magnificent, four-poster double bed, which was particularly funny seeing as we'd only known each other for a year, and only been in each other's company for seven days out of that year.

I soon discovered that the Deborah I'd spent time with in Mazatlán was quite a different Deborah to the one I was now with in Zanzibar. She was passionate about her writing and very focused on getting all the information she needed for her novel. I was conscious that we only had a week together and that there was an awful lot of research to be done. In the event, the whole trip was quite frenetic and rather exhausting – but fun!

Deborah was clearly expecting me to act as a top-notch PA/research assistant and at first I panicked, hoping that I actually had what it took to get the job done to Deborah's standards. She could be quite tough at times, and a bit strict. 'Come on hurry up!' she'd say, as I trotted along behind her with my notebook.

The whole week was spent eating, drinking and sleeping Deborah's story 24/7, and I soon felt as if I knew the characters every bit as well as she did. It really was a non-stop operation and at 4 o'clock in the morning Deborah would regularly shoot up in bed, shake me and cry, 'Oh God, I've got that bit all wrong!'

Oh dear, what now?! I'd think to myself, as Deborah sprung out of bed and started tapping away furiously on her laptop. *Tap, tap, tap* went the keyboard as she muttered, 'Cat, shouldn't have been wearing torn, faded jeans, and she certainly wouldn't have had red lipstick on.' *Tap,*

tap, tap. 'I've definitely done that part all wrong!'
Tap, tap, tap.

Deborah decided that we needed to be familiar with the whole island, and to make that happen we needed a local guide – somebody who could take us round and help us with everything on what we referred to as 'The List'. And a very eclectic list it was! Deborah had very efficiently noted everything we needed to investigate which included: 'the gigolos' or 'beach boys'; the 'seaweed ladies'; a visit to a voodoo shop; and meeting a witch doctor.

However, more on 'The List' later, because before we could really get going, we needed that all-important guide.

We headed straight into Stone Town after breakfast on our first morning to get a sense of the general vibe and see what was going on. As we breezed into a little souvenir shop full of wooden carvings and various bits and bobs, a very smiley local guy popped up from behind the counter and introduced himself as Simba.

'Ooh, look at you, lovely ladies! What can I get for you?' he said, being very charming and charismatic. Deborah and I quietly looked at one another and both had the same idea. *Hum… he's working in his souvenir shop during the day, but he's definitely a gigolo by night,* we decided, and both started laughing at the idea.

Deborah then asked him, 'Can you find somebody to help me? I'm researching the island for a book I'm writing and we need a guide.'

Simba, who was immediately very taken with the idea, started dancing round the shop saying, 'I'll help! I'll help! I can help you *all* week. I'll do whatever you want me to do and I'll take you wherever you need to go.'

In her typical American way, Deborah calmly said, 'Okay then Simba, let's make a deal. Yes, we'd like you to be with us all week, but we *don't* need you to take your clothes off!'

Simba was clearly very taken aback at being told to remain clothed – clearly a first for him – nevertheless, he agreed to accompany us for the whole week. True to his word, he proved to be a very willing guide, and quite a sight with his wonderful, huge smile and dreadlocks threaded with multicoloured beads. Despite promising to remain fully clothed, however, he was always desperate to whip off his shirt at any and every opportunity to show us his six-pack: walking along the beach, in a bar, sitting in a restaurant. To his credit, he worked really hard to entice us, but needless to say, didn't succeed.

The first item on 'The List' was understanding more about 'the gigolos'. These are the 'beach boys' who target Western women in particular, looking to wine, dine (and anything and everything in between!) for as long as possible. Having met Simba, we felt we'd already ticked that box.

Number two on the list was a visit to the 'seaweed ladies'. Simba agreed to take us to see these women who live in a small village, close to a vast, isolated, and very beautiful beach, where they make their living harvesting and drying seaweed to sell. Deborah and I spent a morning with them, sitting in the water, pruning and picking the seaweed while we listened to their stories. We then watched as they dragged the really long, heavy trails of seaweed for miles across the beach, back to their village, where they hang it out to dry on washing lines. Once dried, the seaweed is broken down and packed into plastic bags, ready for selling in the local shops and at the market.

The third thing on our list was visiting a voodoo store. This was quite scary. Inside it was very dark, dusty, and busy. The entrance was draped with long strips of fur and dried up pieces of bone. Inside, a local man stood behind a counter surrounded by all kinds of interesting charms and potions, promising cures for everything from aches and pains to anxiety. It was a fascinating, weird, and crazy place

Next, we spent time in the slave museum and, of course, the spice markets. The local people are all highly superstitious and Deborah was keen to learn more about the different spirits that play such a significant role in the local culture. There are even certain roads that people refuse to travel, believing that evil spirits are hiding in the trees, waiting to cause harm to the unsuspecting traveller.

Our final port of call was a visit to a witch doctor. This proved to be by far the strangest item on our list. Simba made all the arrangements and came with us on the day; it was really funny because the witch doctor was adamant that Simba had an evil spirit and needed protection. There was always a lot of talk about that sort of thing.

Deborah and I each had our own ceremony with the witch doctor, who said he wanted to prepare protection spells for us which he would write down for us to keep. It was incredible watching him writing away with what looked like gold leaf on brown parchment paper. He drew various lines and symbols, with Deborah's spell coming out looking quite different to mine.

Eventually he said, 'I need to prepare, pray, and spend some more time working on these, so come back to me at the end of the week. In the meantime, I need you to find something special to put the spells in.'

So off we went and found a small jewellery shop where we bought identical little silver cylinders, each with a tiny lid, which looked perfect for the job. When we took these back to the witch doctor, he folded the spells up as many times as he could before pushing them into our cylinders and sealing the lids. He then made us promise to always wear them around our necks for protection.

Deborah was really pleased that we'd managed to tick off everything on the list, although by the end of the week I was exhausted. I hadn't realised quite how full on it was going to be, but then that's all part of the fun of accepting an invitation then going along with everything and living in the moment.

It was wonderful just being with Deborah, who was so passionate about her novel. Throughout the week she moved fast and spoke even faster. 'What do you think of this?' she'd say. 'Does this sound right? Should we change it?' Simba was brilliant in that he became really involved with the story as well, although unfortunately he managed to revert to full 'gigolo mode' by the end of the week.

I should have seen it coming when, one afternoon as we were saying our goodbyes for the day, he sidled up to me and said, 'Oh Jayne, don't you think I should have your phone number for WhatsApp, just in case I can't get in touch with Deborah?'

'Yeah, okay fine,' I said, without really thinking.

What a mistake! From then onwards, after we'd left him for the day and gone to bed, my phone would ping in the middle of the night with a message from him saying: 'Hey… What ya doin'? Why don't you leave Deborah and come and meet me on the beach? I've got something really exciting to show you!'

Sighing deeply, I'd reply, 'Simba, go away. It's late and I need to sleep. I'll see you in the morning.'

Simba turned out to be harder to shake off than I'd anticipated, he even came back to haunt me at my garden salon in the depths of Wiltshire. One of my regular clients had come in for a colour, and I'd just started work on her roots when she said – as all my clients do – 'Jayne! You must tell me about your adventures in Zanzibar. How was Deborah? What did you get up to?'

Well, that particular client was nearly on the receiving end of more than she bargained for! 'I've got some great pictures I can show you,' I said, 'bear with me a moment,' and I popped out to the kitchen to grab my iPad with all my photographs. As I trotted back in, flicking the photos across the screen as I went, I was suddenly, and *very* unexpectedly, confronted with the image of the biggest, blackest erect willy you could imagine!

What the...??! I thought, utterly shocked. Beneath it was a message from Simba saying, 'Hi babe, do you remember me?'

Luckily I was standing behind my client at this point, so I was able to hurriedly delete the image and compose myself, while she stared innocently into the mirror. I could so easily have just handed her the iPad without checking. The very thought still makes my blood run cold! Can you imagine? *Oh Jayne, that looks like an exciting holiday,* she would probably have said politely!

Later that evening I sent the picture to Deborah, 'Look at this from Simba!' I wrote. 'What *is* he on?!'

'Thank God we didn't get involved with that!' she replied.

~ 20 ~

RWANDAN GORILLAS
IN THE MIST

Deborah and I had so much in common, with her setting up salons in Afghanistan whilst I was doing the same in Africa. During our week together in Zanzibar, she told me that she wanted to visit my second academy, the one we'd set up later in Kigali, Rwanda.

'I'd love to meet the students, see what you're doing and maybe work with you for a day, learning about the history,' she said. So much of the history in the area is tied up with the genocide and is incredibly traumatic, but it was something she wanted to understand more about. 'Once we've done that,' she continued, 'there's something really special I'd like to do. It's my 57th birthday and I've always wanted to see the mountain gorillas. That would certainly make it the holiday of a lifetime!'

'Sure,' I said confidently, quietly thinking, *I probably need to research this!*

But in the event, that's exactly what we did – and Deborah was right, it really *was* the experience of a lifetime.

Nigel, who had been keen to meet Deborah, said that he would come along on the gorilla trip, bringing Pie with him. It was all arranged, with Deborah and I flying from Zanzibar to Nairobi, where we met up with Nigel and Pie before going onto a house we had in Kigali. I spent some time showing Deborah the academy and the salons there, before we all left for our 'gorilla expedition' up the mountain!

We travelled the three hours north of Kigali by taxi, ending up close to the border with the Congo. When we finally arrived at our accommodation – well, I have to admit it left quite a bit to be admired and I could tell that Nigel, who was very much used to living the high life, wasn't impressed. However, once he was over his huffing and puffing, and all his, 'I don't want to bloody well stay here!' everything was fine. True, the hotel was a bit shabby, with rather raggedy décor and shabby furniture, but the staff were all very good and the food was okay; plain, with a lot of rice, but we didn't mind.

We were up very early on the morning of the gorilla trip. There were just eight of us visitors, along with two guides. We were told there were 13 gorilla families living on the vast mountain, and the trackers went off ahead to seek them out. Once they locate a gorilla family, the trackers radio back to the guides and the adventure begins. Luckily for us, it wasn't too long before word came of a sighting… and we were off!

The terrain was quite steep in places and we trekked for the best part of two and a half hours without seeing anything. At times, the guides, who had machetes, would be hacking through the undergrowth and cutting back the bamboo so that we could get through. We certainly weren't trekking along a regular tourist route.

Up and up we went, deep into the jungle, being as quiet as possible. It was hard-going and we were all starting to get a bit tired, especially Deborah who grumbled, 'I knew I should have lost two stone before I did this trip.'

Then suddenly the guide ahead of us turned and put his finger to his lips: 'Shh…,' he whispered, 'They're just around the corner.'

And there they were: about ten gorillas in total, including an enormous, 45-year-old gorilla known locally as the 'President'. There were some female gorillas close by and lots of toddlers, who were literally playing together, just like our little people do.

We were allowed to spent an hour in the company of these amazing animals and, oh my goodness, it was the shortest hour of my life.

The gorillas didn't seem to mind our being there and just sitting so close to them was simply incredible. They weren't aggressive at all, although the guide told us that by about 11 or 12 o'clock in the morning, they are usually a bit 'merry' from having chewed so much bamboo. Apparently, the sap has the effect of making them feel a bit drunk, so they were very chill.

I never once felt afraid in the company of these gentle giants, although at one point the President, who had been lying on his back, very mellow, suddenly woke up and started moving towards us. It was an incredible moment, like watching King Kong rise up before us.

'What the fuck?!' shrieked Deborah, although we weren't really worried as the guides who were with us understood the gorillas and knew how to handle them.

One thing that really impressed me about the whole trip was knowing that the number of visitors is heavily restricted. Expeditions up the mountain are kept to very small groups and trips are only permitted a maximum of three times a year. This means that the excursion is very expensive, but we thought, *Who cares?!*

It was magical and the memory of that day will stay with me for the rest of my life, so it was worth every penny.

~ 21 ~

BALI
(MY HAPPY PLACE)

Bali is my all-time favourite place in the world which I first visited when I was 25, and working on *Sea Goddess*. Sharon, who worked with me in the salon and became a very good friend of mine, took me for that lovely cocktail at the beautiful Amandari hotel. Back then, I had sat by the infinity pool looking out at the lush, tropical landscape, telling myself that one day, when I could afford it, I would return to Bali and stay there.

That day came 25 years later in 2015, when we returned for Nigel's 60th birthday. We had never been to Bali as a family – virtually all our time overseas had been spent in Africa – so I thought it would be the perfect place for a special visit and birthday celebration – and it was.

We stayed in stunning Airbnb villas, travelling round the island, sightseeing and generally soaking up the unique, spiritual atmosphere of calm and serenity, which was wonderful.

The big surprise, however, came on Nigel's actual birthday, when he discovered that I'd booked us all into the Amandari for the night. It was just magical and I simply couldn't believe I was back there; I could almost see the shadow of my 25-year-old self, chatting away to Sharon with our cocktails by the infinity pool. Pie absolutely loved it, while Nigel felt quite overwhelmed by the whole place, and really spoilt.

Needless-to-say, Nigel and Pie both fell in love with Bali, so we went back again the following year. This time, we did all sorts of new and wonderful things, like swimming with dolphins.

A favourite book of mine is *Eat, Pray, Love* by Elizabeth Gilbert, which I'd read about four times by the time we visited Bali again. In her memoir, Elizabeth spends the last three months of her journey of self-discovery in Bali. I had the book with me while we were there on holiday and was reading the part where she decides to visit a spiritual healer, when I decided that was exactly what I needed to do.

In *Eat, Pray, Love* Elizabeth Gilbert meets with a very elderly and wise spiritual healer called the Medicine Man, an idea that I was very drawn towards, but didn't quite know how to achieve. In the event, I started chatting to a local guy called Wyan, who came every morning to look after the swimming pool. To cut a long story short, he did some digging for me and discovered that the Medicine Man in Elizabeth Gilbert's book had sadly died just three weeks before I arrived on the island. However, he told me he knew of somebody else who could help, and offered to take me to meet him.

Naturally I accepted, and the very next afternoon Wyan arrived on his motorbike to whisk me away. I was so excited, feeling like my own version of Julia Roberts in the movie of the book as I climbed on the back of his motorbike.

Then we were off, with my hair blowing freely behind me and the warmth of the sun on my face. *How dreamy is this?* I thought, in my sparkly sandals and Gucci sunglasses with my multicoloured silk kaftan streaming on the breeze behind us.

'Hold on tight, and don't move around too much,' said Wyan, as we bobbed, ducked and dived through the chaotic traffic. Half an hour later, with the noise and busyness of Canggu melting away in our wake, we began climbing high up into the mountains; swirling and zigzagging across the rice fields.

Eventually we arrived at what felt like a small, local village meeting square. It was very quiet and dusty as we climbed off the motorbike, watched closely by a couple of bored cockerels. A wild Bali dog stretched out lazily in the shade beneath a rickety table, laden with the beautifully decorated daily offerings to the Hindu gods. There was not another soul around.

'Do you think we're at the right place, Wyan?' I whispered.

'I hope so,' he replied. 'Let me see if I can find anyone.'

Then, as if from nowhere, Dedi appeared; young, serene, and very wise, he was dressed from head to foot in white robes with brown beads around his neck. He smiled warmly as he greeted us, bowing his head with his palms pressed together in a namaste pose.

Wow! I thought.

'Good afternoon, Jayne,' he said, gently leading me into a dark, candlelit thatched hut where we sat cross-legged opposite each other. White sage incense sticks were smouldering away in the background and a wonderful, deeply cleansing fragrance began to envelop me.

'Do you live in this village?' I asked him.

'No,' he replied. 'I've travelled two hours to meet you here. This is my healing place.'

Dedi had prepared an offering for my ceremony, consisting of a silver plate covered in pink petals and rice. As he took my hands in his he said, 'So Jayne, what can I do for you?'

I had no idea how or where to begin, and as I tried to stutter out a few words, I suddenly felt quite vulnerable and wobbly in the serene, deeply loving and caring environment.

Taking his cue from my uncertainty, Dedi continued, 'I shall perform a purification and energy-boosting ceremony for you, because I feel this is what you really need.'

The next hour was filled with prayer, mantras, humming, chimes and chanting. I had no idea what was being said. *Maybe he's talking in Sanskrit?* I thought. Not that it mattered. Dedi's words were so comforting and so enchanting that I closed my eyes and immediately felt the constant chatter in my mind fade away as I relaxed. For the very first time in my life, I felt totally present and totally in the *now*.

'Jayne, I feel that you, too, are a healer,' he said.

Gosh, I thought, *I've been told that before!*

'You are like me,' he continued. 'We have been together before in a past life. I believe, in fact, that you were my mother.'

Crikey! It was amazing as I, too, had felt there was an incredible bond – a high and energetic vibration – between us.

'Today we become family again,' he said. 'I knew I had to meet with you, Jayne, because as I am healing you, you are healing me.' His chocolate brown eyes stared deep into my soul as he continued, 'The door has been locked, but now I give you the key. You are free; free from your too many worries and anxieties. You make so much stress for yourself. You try to look after too many people and worry far too much. Now, you must do what *you* want to do.'

He then blew on a large horn and began trickling holy water from a silver jug over the crown of my head, which ran down my cheeks and mingled with my salty tears.

I could easily have sat there with Dedi for hours and hours, but sadly the time had come for us to say our farewells. He gave me a huge hug, then placed the beads from around his neck over my head and handed me a box of sandalwood incense sticks.

'We will meet again one day, Momma,' he said.

'I hope so,' I replied. 'I really do hope so.'

As Wyan and I began our journey back to the south of the island, I felt so free; so at peace and without a care in the world. All the colours around me seemed somehow brighter, more vibrant and luminous. As the magical sunset spread across the horizon, far out at sea, I felt this day had been a blessing and that I truly was living the dream.

* * *

But the story didn't end there because I did, indeed, see Dedi again, although it was not until seven years' later… and in the most unlikely of settings – Southampton docks!

Ahead of a trip I had planned to Bali with my new partner Andrew, I contacted Dedi to see how he was, and what he'd been doing.

'I'm fine Momma,' he replied.

I told him I was returning to Bali in October and asked whether he would be there. Dedi said that sadly, he wasn't going to be in Bali at that time as he was soon off on a cruise ship, teaching yoga for several months. When I asked him where he was meeting the ship, he said, 'Southampton.'

'What?!' I replied. 'That's just around the corner from where I live!' I couldn't believe it. We made a plan to meet for coffee and I was absolutely thrilled at the prospect of seeing him again.

~ 22 ~

A NEW START

Back at home following our trip to Bali, it was clear that things between me and Nigel were becoming more and more strained. Our home life together was difficult and I was feeling uneasy, unsettled, and sometimes quite unhappy. As time passed, it became clear that the amazing business rapport and work ethic that we'd always shared wasn't enough to hold us together, and the inevitable cracks started to appear in our relationship.

However – and this is a really important point – despite the unhappy times that resulted in us parting ways, I've always retained a huge amount of respect for Nigel from a work point of view. We made a brilliant team, he and I; Nigel with his sales and numbers; me with my hairdressing and training skills. At the end of the day, however, we simply didn't share enough common ground for our marriage to stay the course forever.

Pie started her 'A' Level course at Winchester in 2016 and I decided to stay close at hand during this period, like a lot of mommies would in my situation, wanting to see her through her exams as safely and as happily as possible.

Just before Pie was due to leave for university, my lovely friend Jillie, whom I've known for about 23 years, came to see me at my salon and asked how I was doing.

'I'm alright,' I told her. 'Not great… but I'm okay.'

I find it intriguing how things have a habit of coming together just at the right time, because three weeks later, when I knew that I really wasn't alright, Jillie sent me a text message: 'How are you doing?' she asked. 'Are you still okay?'

This time I replied, 'No, not really.'

'Maybe you need some time out?' she offered. 'One of my holiday cottages is free if you feel you need to escape for a while.'

My first thought was, *Oh my God, surely I can't?!* The idea terrified me, but then my fighting spirit kicked in: *Feel the fear and do it anyway,* I told myself.

I packed my bags, throwing in my scissors, clothes, shoes, candles, crystals, incense sticks and a few books, and jumped into my Mini. Putting my foot down, I sped off over the hill to where Jillie lives.

As I pulled up, she was there with the front door open, waiting for me. 'I've sorted it all out for you, Jayne,' she said, as she led me inside. 'Look, we can move the table and chairs and put them over here... and the dining area can become your salon; we can put a little backwash in.'

I smiled the moment I walked into Jillie's cottage – where I'm still living now – because it really did feel like I was on holiday. Although I was standing there, shaking at the enormity of what I'd done; and what I was about to do, Jillie made it all seem so straightforward. *Maybe, just maybe,* I thought to myself, *this really will work!?*

Leaving Nigel, and my home, was the hardest thing I've ever done. He was away in Dubai when I left, and although I'd told him I was thinking of going and that we both needed time out, he didn't really believe that I would leave. 'What do you mean?' he's said when I told him. 'Where do you think you're going? You've got your salon here.'

'I can do hair anywhere,' I'd replied.

The first few weeks by myself were pretty scary. There were many mornings when I woke up alone and thought, *I can't do this… I don't want to get up.* But it turned out that I *could* do it – and am still doing it, four years later.

Nigel and I were eventually divorced. It's been a difficult journey to get where I am today, which is happily settled in my own little retreat. Along the way, I've been supported by some very special people, one of whom is Roisin. I first met her just five weeks after I jumped in my Mini with my scissors and my suitcase, leaving my old life behind me.

One morning, around mid-November in 2018, a client came to my salon and said 'Oh my God, Jayne! I've just met the most extraordinary lady. Her name's Roisin and she's a spiritual healer.'

'Wow,' I said. 'Where is she?'

It turned out Rosin was just 10 minutes away from me in a village called Ludwell, near

Shaftesbury. 'I think you should go and see her, because you'd absolutely love her,' my client said.

Intrigued, and more than a little curious, I called Roisin to make an appointment. I was still feeling quite raw, having left Croft Cottage and my old life behind me, although I had no idea what Roisin could possibly do to make things better.

It was a Saturday morning when I rocked up at her house. The front door opened and there stood a beautiful Scottish lady in her mid-60s, with lovely, twinkly blue eyes and a very kind smile.

'Hi Jayne. Come in, come in,' she said in her soft, Scottish accent.

She led me upstairs to her treatment room, then suddenly stopped and turned to look at me. 'You're a very special person, aren't you?' she said, carefully examining my face. *Am I? I certainly don't feel like a particularly special person right now,* I thought, and I wondered if it was just a kind comment she made to everyone who came to see her.

Roisin's treatment room was like a cosy cave. The treatment couch, which had a big, bright purple amethyst underneath, was surrounded by candles. As I lay down, she said softly, 'So, tell me about you. How are you?' And with that I burst into tears.

The warm, cosy, womb-like environment seemed to bring all my emotions to the surface and everything came pouring out. 'Oh my goodness!' said Roisin, obviously a little taken aback at my sudden rush of feeling,

'Oh Roisin,' I sobbed, 'I've just turned the whole of my life upside down in the last five weeks.'

My head was bursting with negative, depressed thoughts, so it was amazing when Roisin simply took my hands and said, 'But look at what you've done. We should be celebrating this! Look at your courage and your bravery. You're finding yourself at last.'

She then wrapped me up, all lovely and warm, and gave me this wonderful Reiki treatment. Again, it wasn't something I understood or knew anything about, but the process felt very soothing and healing.

After an hour, we sat back down together and talked through a few things. 'Tell me, Jayne,' she said, 'did you actually see or feel anything during the treatment?'

I described how, at one stage, I'd seen thousands of brightly coloured butterflies in my mind's eye, floating above me in the room. 'That's a sign of a transformation coming,' said Roisin.

Sometime later, when I thought about that comment, it reminded me of a story Deborah had told me, when she too had left her old life behind and started again. Like me, she one day packed all her precious belongings into her Mini, along with her cats, leaving her life in LA for a fresh start in Mazatlán. I remembered Deborah telling me how she'd just thought, *I love Mazatlan, I'm going to drive all the way down the west coast and create a new life for myself there,* and that, as she drove into town, she'd seen literally hundreds of beautifully coloured butterflies flutter across the road in front of her. It's also something she wrote about in her book, *Carnival Street*.

I floated out of Roisin's house that Saturday morning and drove the few minutes back to my cottage. Strangely, by the time I arrived home, I realised I was absolutely exhausted; I think it was probably all part of the treatment. I slept for 24 hours straight, waking only to drink gallons of water every so often as I was so very thirsty. Again, this was probably part of the healing, detox, cleansing and clearing. Once I'd come to after my marathon sleeping session, I was fully back to life and bouncing.

Roisin has since become a very close friend of mine and I've even studied Reiki 1 and Reiki 2 with her. Every so often, she'll say to me, 'You do realise you're a healer, don't you Jayne?' and I'll think, *Oh, here we go again.* However, I do wonder if one day my career will take a more spiritual path? Perhaps I'll be 'The Healing Hairdresser'?

Perhaps I already am.

ANDREW 'THE FOX'

Fast forward two years to March 2021, and we were in another 'lockdown'; me in a 'bubble' – that strange language that became so familiar – with three girlfriends, Jill (a very entertaining South African lady), Jillie (who I rent the cottage from) and Justine, all of whom live close-by. Feeling bored one weekend, I decided to host a 'Prosecco evening' at the cottage so we could sit by the fire, enjoy a few drinks and share some gossip.

On the night, the girls all rocked up for fizz and chatter, with Jill announcing that she'd brought her Botox kit along if anyone fancied a jab (I decided not to get involved in that one!). After a few drinks, Jill, having declared herself to be the all-time on-line dating specialist, suddenly said, 'For Christ's sake, Jayne, you've been here in the cottage on your own now for two and a half years, I think it's time you got back in the saddle!'

Oh God, I thought, *I'm not ready for that yet…* Nevertheless, as the night wore on and the glasses were topped up, the girls decided that, between them, they were going to start this particular journey for me.

'We're going to do this right now,' said Jill. 'Pass me your iPad, I know just the dating site to use.' And with that she set to, logging into 'Eharmony' and opening up an account for me. She was clearly unstoppable, and so, being tired and rather Prosecco'ed out by now, I gave up and went with the flow.

It turned out that Eharmony was an easy dating site to use as you don't need to write a full-blown profile about yourself, which I personally think is an awful thing to have to do as it feels like writing a sales pitch. To finish off, we found a couple of photographs that I was relatively happy with, added those to the account and then, before I had a chance to voice any kind of protest, Jill had pressed the button. It was that easy – I'd gone live!

The girls left at about 11 o'clock that night, at which point I just about managed to stagger upstairs and crawl into bed. When I woke the next morning, my first thought was, *Oh God, don't move your head... this really is a terminal hangover...* as I made my way downstairs. Then the memories of the night before started filtering back and, in a sudden 'Bridget Jones' moment, my second thought was, *Oh my God! What have I done? What did we do?* I made a coffee, grabbed my iPad, and sat down to steady my nerves as I logged in.

I was so anxious that it took me a few moments to remember my password; when I did, and tapped on the Eharmony inbox, a notification appeared telling me that I had seven messages. Hilariously, I thought, *Wow, check me out! I've only been live for a few hours!* Scrolling through the inbox I spotted the name Andrew – and clicked: *Humm? Looks promising...* I thought. Up popped a message saying, 'Hi Jayne, how are you? I just read your profile; it sounds really interesting.'

I then tapped on Andrew's profile and a handful of photographs popped up. I had a flick through them and it was weird, because there he was, in so many places that I'd visited over the years, including Barbados, London and Africa. I decided that he looked kind, with a lovely smile.

Once I'd got to know Andrew, we had a real 'Sliding Doors' moment when we realised that, not only had we visited the same countries and cities, we'd also been in the same shops and restaurants. It transpired that the Christmas I'd worked at Harrods on the fifth floor, Andrew had been on the second floor with his children, queuing up to visit Father Christmas. Such an incredible co-incidence!

We also realised that he was living in Barbados at exactly the same time I was visiting with the cruise ship, all those years ago. We often wonder if there were times I walked into a spoily restaurant there, just as he was walking out. Maybe he held the door open for me? Or perhaps he was on the beach just a few umbrellas away. We'll never know, but it's fun to think about and I find all the possibilities intriguing.

I responded to Andrew's message on the Eharmony site and we started chatting. After a few exchanges, we swapped mobile phone numbers and really started talking; sometimes for hours and hours. Andrew, being such a chatterbox, made the whole thing so easy. We were still in lockdown at this point and weren't able to meet in person, but in some ways that was good as we had so much time to just chat. By the time we actually met in person we felt as if we'd know each other for ever.

Two years on and Andrew and I are still talking and talking… and loving each other's company. I call him 'the fox' as in 'the silver fox' because of his white hair.

Bali, which holds a very special place in my heart, turned out to be somewhere Andrew had never visited. Strangely, in recent months I'd been experiencing a strong sense of wanting to return there. I know that Andrew, being a spiritual person like me, would love it there and the more I thought about it, the more I decided we needed to go. The only drawback, however, was the cost of the flights: *If we go for two weeks,* I kept thinking, *it's going to be very expensive.*

Then something fortuitous, and very unexpected, happened – you might call it a manifestation! Every month I check my premium bonds, and most months I win a small prize of around £25 or £50, but on the day I calculated how much money I'd need to visit Bali again, I was amazed to find that was the exact amount that I'd won. *Thank you, universe!*

Andrew and I are off to Bali in October, which I'm very excited about. Not to the Amandari Hotel this time. That was a beautiful chapter in my life, but now it's time to make new memories.

~ 24 ~

REFLECTIONS

My mom and I had always dreamt of going away on holiday together, just the two of us for some special, girlie time. Sadly, for one reason or another, that never happened. Time ran away… then ultimately ran out for us.

I'd always dreamt about me and Pie taking a little trip together one day, when she was old enough to sip cocktails and we could party the night away! I'd also promised myself that, having worked on board so many cruise ships, I would one day float from deck to deck in a sparkly cocktail dress, sailing off to exotic ports of call – as a guest.

Both dreams came true in October 2022. I don't think either of us had ever been *so* excited! We embarked *Queen Victoria,* one of Cunard's very smart, top-drawer cruise liners, in Southampton on a damp and blustery Thursday afternoon.

Our cabin was to die for; large and airy with a huge double bed and a welcoming, chilled, ready-to-sip bottle of champagne. Pie immediately cracked it open and we sat out on our balcony pondering what cocktail dress to adorn ourselves in for the evening ahead.

We spent the next four days laughing, joking and floating around the ship in our fluffy white dressing gowns, moving between the spa to the champagne bar, and 'repeat'!

It was such a special time and, as my dad would say, 'Certainly one for the memory banks!'

* * *

My memory bank now overflows with the most glorious images, stories and reminders of times like these, all of which spring from my being a hairstylist, which, for me, was – and continues to be – the greatest occupation ever.

I would like to say a huge thank you to everyone who has trusted me with their locks, and beautiful manes. I don't have clients, you are all my special friends. We share our stories, laughter – and sometimes tears – between the shampooing, snipping and hair colouring. I feel humbled and extremely blessed by all of that and everything in between. Thank you!

We may not have it ALL together, but together we have it all.

And Pie… know well and forever, I love you so very much. God bless.

Deborah's 'Tippy Toes' salon in Mexico

With Deborah in Zanzibar

Jayne McCarthy

ZANZIBAR ALBUM
Fishing boats; 'Seaweed lady'; Simba with Deborah;
Simba at the market; Simba

Left: With Deborah outside our botel in Stone Town

Right: The witch doctor working on our protection spells

Jayne McCarthy

Left: Rwandan gorillas in the mist - with Deborah and Pie

Right: On the Queen Victoria with Pie

Left: With Pie on the Queen Victoria

244

SCRAPBOOK

Jayne McCarthy

Life is a great adventure... go and live it!

There is freedom waiting for you,
On the breezes of the sky,
And you ask 'What if I fall?'
Oh but my darling,
What if you fly?

Erin Hanson

Remember Her?

Somewhere inside of you, there's a little firecracker with her arms folded and a frown on her face.

She isn't happy about all the times you said no when you wanted to say yes.

All the times you said yes when you wanted to say no.

She wanted you to buy the ticket.

She wanted you to take that trip.

She definitely wanted you to take that risk – the one that may have just opened a whole new world.

She wants you to remember what it feels like to run to the sea without a care in the world and splash and laugh until you ache.

To face the day without a fear in your heart and embrace every opportunity that comes.

She doesn't understand why you won't wear the bikini.

She doesn't understand why you won't eat the cake.

She doesn't understand why you don't let it go.

She definitely doesn't understand why you accept second best.

Somewhere inside there is a little girl who wonders at the adult you've become.

She still has many things she wants to learn and so many people still to meet.

She still has food she'd like to taste and parties she wants to dance at.

She still has places she wants to visit and wonders she wants to stare at.

Somewhere inside you, there is a little firecracker,desperate to see more of this thing we call life.

Go get her, she's fun.

Donna Ashworth
Poem from: *To the Women, words to live by* (Lulu: 2020)

Printed in Great Britain
by Amazon

38695078R00145